BY THE BOOK?

BY THE BOOK?

CONTEMPORARY PUBLISHING IN AUSTRALIA

EDITED BY EMMETT STINSON

MONASH University
Publishing

Monash University Publishing
Building 4, Monash University
Clayton, Victoria 3800, Australia
www.publishing.monash.edu

Monash University Publishing brings to the world publications which advance the best traditions of humane and enlightened thought.
Monash University Publishing titles pass through a rigorous process of independent peer review.

National Library of Australia Cataloguing-in-Publication entry:

 Author: Stinson, Emmett, editor.

 Title: By the Book? Contemporary Publishing in Australia

 ISBN: 9781922235206 (paperback)

 Series: Publishing

 Notes: Includes bibliographical references.

 Subjects: Publishers and publishing--Australia; Publishers and publishing; Electronic publishing--Australia; Book industries and trade--Australia.

 Dewey Number: 070.50994

 www.publishing.monash.edu/books/bb-9781922235206.html

Design: Les Thomas

Printed in Australia by Griffin Press an Accredited ISO AS/NZS 14001:2004 Environmental Management System printer.

The paper this book is printed on is certified by the Programme for the Endorsement of Forest Certification scheme. Griffin Press holds PEFC chain of custody SGS - PEFC/COC-0594. PEFC promotes environmentally responsible, socially beneficial and economically viable management of the world's forests.

CONTENTS

III. PUBLISHING LITERATURE

INTRODUCTION

Emmett Stinson

Over the last two years, the Australian publishing industry has been characterised by a turbulence that has disrupted several decades of more or less uninterrupted growth.[1] Up until 2011 – when REDgroup retail, the owners of Borders and Angus & Robertson went into administration – the steady expansion of Australian publishing[2] made it one of the most successful national cultural industries. In 2007, for example, the book industry produced more income than 'music and theatre production and arts festivals combined' (Carter and Galligan 2007, 1). Although all of the largest Australian publishers – with the exception of Allen & Unwin – were technically owned by overseas companies, these multinationals had significant commercial and cultural investments in publishing local work. The major publishers employed significant numbers of staff for editing, production control, design, sales, marketing and public relations. They had also invested heavily in infrastructure for the storage and distribution of books, and subsidised much of the local printing industry.

The economic and cultural activity of these larger companies was buttressed by a vibrant and diverse independent publishing sector that arose during the last two decades. These smaller publishers often utilised the distribution systems of the larger publishing houses, who disseminated their works for a percentage of recommended retail price, and thus enabled them to access the broader Australian market. Some smaller publishers, such as Giramondo and Sleepers Publishing, focused on producing 'high' cultural literary works that went on to win major national awards.[3] Other larger, 'mid-level' independents – such as Text, Scribe, Lonely Planet, and Hardie Grant, among others – became an important force within the industry. Text

---

[1] There were, however, some setbacks to the industry as a result of the introduction of GST in 2000 (Lee et al. 2009, 7).

[2] However, while the book industry grew by an average of 1.6 per cent per annum from 2000 to 2010, this level of growth actually suggests that the book industry underperformed in comparison to similar industries (Book Industry Strategy Group 2011, 17).

[3] For example, Giramondo published Alexis Wright's *Carpentaria* (2006), which won the Miles Franklin Award in 2007. Sleepers Publishing published Steven Amsterdam's *Things We Didn't See Coming* (2009), which won *The Age* Book of the Year in 2009.

and Scribe, in particular, frequently competed with the major Australian houses to sign the best-known literary authors, while also publishing books that had a significant commercial impact. By 2009, the whole publishing industry was responsible for employing some 5000 workers directly, and thousands more across the supply-chain of printing, distribution, and book sales (Lee et al. 2009, 10).

All of this local growth, however, was largely underpinned by a copyright scheme that enabled Australian publishers to subsidise the production of local works with income derived from republishing books initially printed overseas. The copyright act of 1968 was amended in 1991 to protect Australian publishers from overseas competition in a provision known as the 30/90-day rule:

> Under the existing system, parallel importation restrictions (PIRs) provide for a 30/90-day rule, based on a 'use it or lose it' principle. If a book is published overseas, local publishers have 30 days to produce a local edition; if no action is taken, the book may be 'parallel imported'. Once a book has been published in Australia, the publisher is given up to 90 days to replenish stock, before parallel importation applies. (Book Industry Strategy Group 2011, 12)

Re-publishing overseas titles is a comparatively cheap and low-risk venture. Not only do high sales overseas frequently correspond with high sales in Australia, but also already-published overseas works do not need to be substantively re-edited, which removes a significant cost from publishing a title. The 30/90-day rule thus effectively gave Australian publishers a reliable and protected income stream, which could be used to cross-fund local works, which have been historically unlikely to turn a significant profit,[4] and often fail even to recoup the costs of their production.

The first cracks in this system began to appear in 2009, when an Australian Productivity Commission recommended that PIRs be removed and the 30/90-day rule abolished. This productivity commission had already proven divisive among sectors of the industry. Booksellers strongly advocated for the removal of PIRs, but publishers were wary of any changes that might undermine their hegemony over the local market. While publishers were

---

[4]   'The fiction bestsellers in paperback surveyed from 1983 to 1999 show clearly that many overseas authors but very few Australian writers have achieved this highly marketable status.' (Hegarty 2006, 236).

ultimately successful in convincing the government not to accept the Productivity Commission's recommendation, in retrospect, this proved to be something of a Pyrrhic victory. At the same time that publishers were busy circling their wagons, consumers were changing their behaviour, increasingly lured to purchase print books online at sites like Amazon and The Book Depository, which were exempt from PIR laws and thus offered access to much cheaper overseas editions of foreign works. The global market had arrived in Australia in spite of local copyright restrictions, resulting in a difficult environment for booksellers and publishers that culminated in the collapse of REDgroup, a chain that then comprised nearly 20 per cent of the Australian bookselling market. Although the industry appears to have stabilised somewhat this year, it is still a long way from recovering from these losses.

This industrial turbulence also coincided with the emergence of new methods for digitally disseminating books, the most prominent of which are the ebook and the digital reader. Although ebooks cannot be blamed for the Australian industry's particular difficulties, they illustrate many of the uncertainties and difficulties facing the industry. Ebooks theoretically solve many problems that have hamstrung traditional publishing, since they dispense with print and distribution costs and enable Australian publishers to sell into a global market. In practice, however, the over-whelming majority of the industry's profits still derive from print, but titles must now be prepared for both digital and print formats. Ebooks thus actually represent both another cost and an increase in organisational complexity for most publishers. Moreover, ebooks have required an often fraught renegotiation of basic issues like author royalties, seller agreements, and pricing. In this sense, ebooks have not really provided either a new business model or a particularly significant income stream for most Australian publishers, but have instead complicated and problematised existing models.

For scholars of publishing, this industrial turbulence has been accom-panied by a conceptual turbulence. The changes in the industry have required a re-examination of some of the most foundational issues for the field, as we are forced to ask what constitutes a book in the age of digital distribution, and what a publisher is in an age of widespread self-publishing. Determining where the notion of the book ends and where other forms of digital media begin is rendered extremely problematic given the rise of applications and other software that seem to blur these boundaries. Indeed, some publishers are even beginning to experiment with television production and other forms of media, in an attempt to re-configure themselves as cross-media content producers.[5] The rise of self-publishing and partner-publishing models similarly calls into question the conception of publishing that has existed virtually unchallenged since the end of the nineteenth century. In this older model, publishers and authors shared risk in bringing new work out into the marketplace. Authors took a risk in licensing publishers their intellectual property, while publishers took a risk in absorbing upfront costs (such as advance royalties, editing and printing) that they hoped to recoup in the market. But new digital self-publishing services displace the risk squarely onto the shoulders of authors, an arrangement that is not nearly as advantageous as its strongest advocates claim.[6]

This essay collection represents an attempt to think through the many issues – both commercial and conceptual – that are currently facing Australian publishing. The collection is divided into three separate areas of concern, and the first section, entitled 'Industry Dynamics', attempts to wrestle directly with this large-scale change. Mark Davis's 'Publishing in the End Times' examines the future of Australian publishing by looking back to the key historical role of publishing in establishing public culture and democracy, and arguing that the industry must seek to realign its commercial goals with its core political and social values. Peter Donoughue's 'At War with the Future' argues that most publishers have been hindered by their adherence to older models of thinking and suggests that they can capitalise on their still vital social mission by embracing new modes of distribution to meet the needs of their readers. Tim Coronel's 'What Next for the Australian Book Trade?' takes a pragmatic, industry-practitioner's view of the trade, noting both the many challenges it will face and the essential role of local culture for any future Australian publishing. Finally, in 'Unintended Consequences', Sybil Nolan and Matthew Ricketson chart the dwindling fortunes of literary reviewing pages in the major newspapers and note the dire consequences of this for both the industry and book culture more broadly.

The second section, entitled 'Small Press Publishing', seeks to examine this increasingly visible and vibrant sector of the industry. Caroline Hamilton's

---

[5]   In the United States, Penguin Random House has produced a show entitled, *Heartland Table* for the Food Network (Trachtenberg 2013).

[6]   I have already written on paradigm shift involved in self-publishing elsewhere. *See* Stinson 2011.

'Don't Look Back' charts the continuing success of print literary magazines in order to examine the link between literary entrepreneurship and the widespread belief that technology is an inherently empowering tool. Phillip Edmonds's 'A Democratic Moment – Or More of the Same?', however, considers literary magazines in a very different light, suggesting that the demise of several important print magazines over the last several years represents the end of a 'democratic moment' in Australian publishing. Kevin Brophy's 'A Fragile Craft' highlights the tenuous position of the small press publisher by examining the effects of government funding on an often overlooked area of the industry – poetry publishing. Aaron Mannion and Amy Espeseth's 'Small Press Social Entrepreneurship: The Values of Definition' considers small press publishing in relation to social entrepreneurship models in an attempt to define a sector of the industry that often sits in a liminal space between altruistic desire and commercial concern.

The final section, 'Publishing Literature', examines the essential and even determining relationship that the industry exerts on those works that are subsequently construed as literature. My own essay, 'In the Same Boat', argues that the reception of Australian short story collections provides an essential insight into how both the market and Australian national self-perception continue to shape literary culture. Beth Driscoll's 'Twitter, Literary Prizes and the Circulation of Capital' uses Pierre Bourdieu's sociological theory to examine how social media responses to literary events can provide an illuminating snapshot of the contemporary literary field. Ivor Indyk's 'The Economics of the Australian Literary Classic' responds to recent claims that universities have disregarded 'classic' Australian literature, by arguing that there has always been a disjuncture between the cultural status of 'classic' works and their economic viability. Finally, Sophie Allan and Beth Driscoll's 'Making the List' analyses the influence of literary prizes on educational reading lists, and again applies a Bourdieusian frame to argue for the importance of prizes for female authors, such as the recently established Stella Prize, in ensuring the gender-equality of school reading lists.

The perspectives these essays provide represent an important attempt to wrestle with the changes and contradictions of a publishing industry in convergence. They accomplish this task by thinking beyond the bound-aries of the traditional model that has characterised the last hundred years of publishing, while nonetheless casting a skeptical eye towards claims of digital salvation. It is fitting then, that many of these papers were originally delivered at the inaugural Independent Publishing Conference held by the Small Press Network, a relatively new organisation that remains dedicated to the cultural and political aims implicit in traditional publishing, while attempting to assist small and independent publishers adapt to a changing market.

I. Industry Dynamics

Chapter 1

PUBLISHING IN THE END TIMES

Mark Davis

My title, as I hope is immediately obvious, is meant to be ironic and at the same time not quite ironic. It steals from Slavoj Zizek, and, like his book *Living in the End Times* (2010), is intended not so much as a literal description of events as a critique of the general mood of the times.

There is little evidence to support the idea that we are living in the 'end times' in any literal sense. If 'eschatological apocalyptism', as Zizek argues elsewhere, involves the 'fantasy of a symbolic Last Judgement in which all past accounts will be settled', then rather than proclaim the apocalypse it's better to point to the suspect cultural origins of apocalyptic thinking in evangelical Christian doom-saying (Zizek 2009, 148–9). Yet, in very important ways, we do appear to be living through a kind of 'end times', because many of the traditional cultures and institutions that sustained and defined 'us' as a society are in crisis, whether it be the present crises of journalism or publishing, or the ongoing crisis of Western cultural identity. It's cultural and social worlds that are ending, not the natural world, which is merely in the process of becoming unliveable. And these human-made cultural end times of ours – brought about by technological disruption and the relentless march of markets; by changes in consumer expectations and transformations in the way people read; by transformations in the way everyday products are conceived, manufactured and distributed; by profound shifts in the ways in which ideas and knowledge circulate – are having a significant effect on the publishing industry, such that the assumptions that sustained the industry through the twentieth century have in a few short years become much less viable.

What I'm referring to, in part, is the decline of a certain sort of public culture that was a staple of twentieth-century liberal modernity, which was underpinned by certain specific kinds of information flows and certain kinds of audiences, certain gatekeeping practices, certain editorial mores, certain educational structures and assumptions, and certain relationships between culture and its tastemakers. All these artefacts of liberal modernity now, in so far as they continue to exist, arguably live a kind of half-life, existing as much in cultural memory as in fact.

The onus is on us, then, to understand what has happened. At one level, the answers to such questions are so well-known as to have become the stuff of cliché. With the advent of digital media, what were more or less monadic pathways for the dissemination of knowledge have become plural. What were high barriers to entry have become low barriers to entry. What was carefully curated, more or less one-way traffic in information has become multi-directional traffic, and is more democratic or populist, depending on your point of view. The system that linked each genre to a single technological platform – that linked written journalism to the printed newspaper page, or literature to the printed book page, for example – has broken down such that genre is detached from any specific technology in a new, multi-platform environment. That much is easy. But in this process, publishing business models that have worked for generations have been upended, and the question of how publishers might maintain the previous scale and profitability of their businesses, even as they take up new opportunities, remains largely unanswered.

Meanwhile, there has been something of a revolution in consumer expectations. Readers began to expect information and entertainment for free, or close to it. And, to complicate matters further, this shift in consumer expectations is linked to a shift in understandings of partic-ipatory citizenship. People would appear to be no longer so interested in deliberative, rational-democratic culture of the traditional Enlighten-ment kind. The internet has often been imagined as an enabling platform for a kind of super-democracy, in line with received expectations about the democratic potential of interactive media. Top-down, institutionally-derived power and knowledge of the sort championed by 'old media' were out, and bottom-up, networked power and knowledge were in. Often, as the success of organisations like GetUp!, or the social media under-pinnings of the short-lived Occupy movement and the Arab Spring of 2010–2012 show, the outcome has been promising. Yet no less often precisely the opposite has happened. For all its promise, the internet, rather than resembling a super-democracy, has become something of an ideological battleground for bitterly opposed versions of truth that epitomises the anti-democracy prophesied by Thomas Hobbes when he spoke of 'the war of all against all' – '*Bellum omnium contra omnes*' – which he offers as the alternative to the leviathan of sovereign government.

My intent in what follows isn't to bash technology, but to unpack some of its social effects and think about what they might mean for book publishing. It's important, in fact, *not* to attack technology, because when we attack or champion technological change we often lose sight of deeper social and political shifts taking place in the background. In the case of the Australian book publishing industry, retaining a sense of perspective about the impact of digital media is especially important, because technological change has so often been used as a scapegoat for the current sense of crisis pervading many parts of the industry. The challenges the industry faces are very real. According to Nielsen BookScan Australia, from 2009 to 2012 inclusive, industry revenue from book sales fell from $1.29 billion to $0.98 billion, a contraction of almost 25 per cent, even as the number of titles published has stayed almost unchanged.[1] The average selling price of print books dropped from $19.91 to $17.27 (BookScan 2013).[2] With some notable exceptions, print runs have in general fallen as well. This slump, and the demise of companies such as the REDgroup, owner of the Borders and Angus & Robertson bookselling chains, has been blamed on digital media (Rubbo 2012). In Australia and elsewhere, pundits and industry figures speak seriously of the 'end of the book' at the hands of the ebook (Morrison 2011). Yet the contraction has to some degree been offset by revenue from ebook sales, which appears to be averaging at least 10 per cent, and up to 20 per cent at some publishers. And to suggest that the current malaise is a result of technological change overlooks other important considerations.

In a 2011 article on the Australian film industry, Tom Donald speculated on why recent Australian films have often done poorly at the box office and why their industry market share had dropped 10 per cent in a year (Donald 2011). His answer is straightforward. Consumers have been burnt too many times. For too long, he says, the industry has served up over-hyped but second-rate movies and taken its audience for granted. The book publishing industry might be considered in a similar light. Great books still get published by great publishers. But, by too often overselling and undercooking, over the past two decades or so publishers have arguably chipped away at the

---

[1]   From 2009 to 2012, inclusive, the Nielsen BookScan Australia title count, based on separate ISBNs distributed, rose 1 per cent.

[2]   I would like to gratefully thank Michael Webster of Nielsen BookScan Australia for sales and revenue figures supplied for the writing of this article.

basic value proposition that once inspired many people to buy books. At many publishers (but by no means all), editorial budgets and standards fell (McPhee 2001). More and more books aligned themselves with another, previously successful title, and, in a search for sure-fire hits, too many publisher catalogues became, like movie-house billboards, a sad lexicon of reshakes and remakes. This is *Kitchen Confidential* meets *Underbelly*, as one recent blurb puts it. More books became 'fast-track' titles produced to a tight deadline to meet the market but often with little substance, because author and editor were given little time to develop the manuscript.

At the same time, publishers have been caught up in the loss-leader discounting strategies of discount department chains. The admirable hope was that large quantities of inexpensive books in discount department stores and other non-traditional retail outlets would tempt more people to buy books, expanding the market. Yet the stacks of cut-price books just inside the doorways of Kmart, Big W and Target – and, more recently, Australia Post and Aldi – no doubt sent a straightforward message to many of the reading public, which is that publishers can charge more reasonable prices for books if they so choose. The arrival of online retailers, such as Amazon in the mid-1990s and, since 2004, the United Kingdom-based Book Depository (which was bought by Amazon in 2011), with their very large catalogues of titles at lower-than-Australian prices, has tended to confirm perceptions that Australian books are overpriced. Industry campaigns to counter these perceptions, launched in the lead-up to the release in 2009 of the Productivity Commission's report on the parallel importation of books, have apparently had little effect (Australian Publishers Association 2009). Media commentary, and especially the comments threads of newspaper articles about the industry, are often aggressively in support of the view that books are overpriced (*The Age* 2012; Fels 2009; Page 2011; Rubbo 2012). In hindsight, it's clear that the debate was a public relations disaster. What many publishers saw as a desperate and righteous campaign to save their industry evidently looked to many people like so much special pleading from a protected elite.

Australian publishers face considerable challenges. Publishing is a windfall industry reliant on breakout bestsellers for any significant profit, even as many books barely cover costs. Australian trade publishers average less than 11 per cent pre-tax profit (PricewaterhouseCoopers 2011, 26). The well-known imprints that dominate the market are mostly owned by publicly listed global corporations and tied to the demands of the share market and quarterly earnings forecasts, hence increasing the pressure for undercooked and fast-track books (Thompson 2012, 101–46). Australia has around a fourteenth of the population but the same distances as the US, and therefore higher freight costs and lower economies of scale. Rising ebook sales revenues are cold comfort for Australian booksellers, whose staff members are paid more than double the wages of comparable staff overseas. Most members of the book-buying public don't realise that those stacks of cheap books at their local Target, Kmart or Aldi are loss-leaders sold at up to 75 per cent discount that often bring little return to publishers or authors. And there is little understanding of the economies of scale enjoyed by online retailers. Or that Amazon spent the first decade of its life sacrificing profits in a long, relentless game for market share while battling Google, Facebook and Apple for online ascendency; and that not only do they use their market power to demand wafer-thin margins from publishers (who they appear to see as mere collateral damage in their corporate skirmishes), working conditions in their warehouses are so poor as to have prompted government enquiries (BBC 2013) and comments that working conditions are like 'being in a slave camp' (O'Connor 2013).

Perhaps more than any other factor affecting the industry, the discounting tactics of online retailers have changed pricing perceptions and destroyed much of the value of the industry, yet for many consumers and industry critics, such tactics seem little more than wish fulfilment. In 2010, I chaired a panel on parallel importation at the Melbourne Writers Festival in which non-industry panellists flatly refused to believe that the majority of books in Australia had print runs so low that they barely made any margin. By then it was too late. Like many people, their eyes were apparently fixed on the dump bins of Dan Brown, Harry Potter and bestselling cookbooks in their local discount department store, and they were asking, 'Why aren't all books sold as cheaply as this?' on the apparent presumption that booksellers and publishers are otherwise making a killing.

The Australian book publishing industry disrupted itself, and had been disrupted by outside forces, long before it had to deal with technological disruption from ebooks. So, now that publishers are faced with genuine technological disruption, what might the future hold in these digital 'end times' where people talk seriously about the 'end of the book'?

At a session at the 2012 Book Expo America, a panellist reportedly shouted out, 'Digital is here, get over it.' It wasn't reported as to whether the panellist also offered a viable new business plan for the industry. A common perception within the industry is that to thrive, publishers should simply become channel-agnostic. That is, unhitch content from the old ink-and-paper business model and adopt a multi-channel business model that privileges those platforms where decent returns can be made. In sheer commercial terms, that's probably not such a bad model, though it's not much more than a first step.

The problem with thinking simply in terms of platform-agnostic publishing is that it underestimates the nature of the current transformation in at least two ways. First, since the introduction of the transistor and then the silicon chip, integrated circuit technology has led to the fundamental restructuring of every industry. As early as the 1960s, it had begun to transform the balance of global trade with the rise of Japan as an electronic manufacturing nation, in part because Western nations were slow to remodel their supply chains. More recently, every industry that has been disrupted by digital technology, from the music industry, to newspapers, to pornography, to the video rental industry, has been transformed, not simply because new channels have been added to an existing content-production model, but because the new environment forces business models to change in more profound ways.

In the case of book publishing, simply adding new digital channels to the existing model won't be sufficient, because digital technology profoundly changes the relationship between publishers and authors. The question publishers now have to face is: what are they offering their authors? The mainstay of traditional publishing has been their stranglehold on marketing and distribution. In the digital world they no longer have this power, which is increasingly held by outside firms such as Amazon, Apple and Kobo, which offer services that authors can access directly, and that new authors such as Amanda Hocking and John Locke have used to build six-figure sales (Pilkington 2012). Crucially, publishers have traditionally acted for authors as managers of risk by underwriting the costs of production and by offering authors insurance against commercial failure through the provision of advances. In short, they functioned as quasi-banks. Yet in the digital world, the costs of entry have fallen to a point where they are easily manageable by most authors. In the meantime, publisher advances have shrunk because of changing market conditions. As one UK publisher said, in the midst of news that UK publishers had recently cut advances by as much as 80 per cent, '10K is the new 50K' (Morrison 2011).

Print isn't dead. Far from it. Witness, for example, the sales of the print edition of *Fifty Shades of Grey* versus the ebook version. The ebook version is Amazon's biggest ever seller, and in June 2012 became the first Kindle title to sell over a million copies, while the print version had global sales of over 20 million copies in that same period (*The Independent* 2012). In the United

Kingdom, for example, digital books still only account for 6 per cent of the market (Bower 2012). In the United States, ebook revenues have slowed, and in 2012 made up 23 per cent of publisher revenues, with expectations that they would level out at around 30 per cent (Digital Bookworld 2013). Wherever ebook sales end up, the impact of digital publishing is such that traditional publishers can no longer offer an exclusive service to authors, who now have significantly greater choice and control over their possible routes to readers. Publishers have arguably lost their near monopoly over content, marketing and distribution, and, incidentally, much of their role as cultural gatekeepers. It's this loss of monopoly power, not simply the emergence of ebooks and other new channels, that most destabilises the traditional book publishing business model. No doubt the industry will also consolidate further through mergers to maintain market power and critical mass in the face of competition from new providers such as Amazon, Google and Apple, as Penguin and Random House in 2012 agreed to do. But to thrive, publishers will have to transform their relationship with authors and readers. New business and service models are already emerging that challenge the old and open up new possibilities. An example is Open Road Media, a small digital house – one prepared to innovate not only on technology, but also on such things as flexible pricing – that recently put a backlist literary title by Iris Murdoch into the UK bestseller lists (Gaughran 2012).

The second problem with assuming that merely publishing across all channels will revive the book publishing industry is arguably more profound, and goes to the very definition of what publishing is. The current changes to our technological social worlds aren't merely incremental, such as the addition of new channels to the mediascape. They go to the heart of the definition of the public sphere.

Benedict Anderson is probably the critic who has come closest to under-standing the fundamental link between book publishing, national cultures and civic ideals. Print capitalism, he argues, made the very idea of the nation possible; and with it, we might add, the idea of liberal democracy. Since the seventeenth century, print capitalism has provided a basis for the 'imagined community' of nation, since it provides a sense of common temporal location, common ends and shared cultural objectives, because we understand that when we read a book or a newspaper, so do others who share these interests (Anderson 1991). In the mid-nineteenth century, cultural critics began to consciously weave this logic into the fabric of an emerging secular democratic culture. Matthew Arnold and F. R. Leavis are among those who most famously installed books and literature at the centre of secular modernity, and at the centre of new mass education systems, as a bastion against social 'anarchy' and as a 'civilising influence' for the mercantile middle classes, capable of cohering society in the face of class conflict, mammon and industrialisation (Eagleton 1983). A version of this project was expertly marketed by book publishers, from Bennett Cerf at Random House, to Allen Lane at Penguin Books, who believed that the social and commercial uses of books could be intertwined as part of a broad project of social critique and improvement.

There was much to fault in such projects. The 'great critics' of the early twentieth century no doubt deserve much of the criticism they have famously attracted from Marxists, feminists and other critics of the ethnocentric Western canon. The 'great publishers' of the mid-twentieth century were opportunistically commercial at least as much as they were idealistic. They ran businesses, not charities. My point is that these links between liberal democratic culture and print capitalism helped underwrite an entire cultural system.

A version of this same project operated in Australia. As I've argued elsewhere, Australian publishers helped underpin the extraordinary cultural resurgence that took place between the mid-1960s and the late 1980s as part of a 'cultural mission' that found mass markets for literary writing and books about issues such as feminism and Aboriginal issues (Davis 2010).

As such, publishing provides a foundation for modernity and humanism, and for the liberal social contract. Yet this contract, no less than the economic contract that underpinned print capitalism, is arguably in the process of being radically disrupted. When publishers talk of adding new channels to the existing menu, they seek to repair the broken economic contract between publishers and readers. But this leaves the question of the social contract. When we look at the current transformation of the book publishing industry, we see more than simply technological disruption. What we see is a transformation and crisis in liberalism, in modernity, in humanism, and in the very notion of the public sphere. The current transformation in the way information and knowledge are distributed isn't merely technological, but involves a crisis of elites, a crisis of expert knowledge – witness, for example, the anti-scientific undermining of the scientific consensus on global warming – a crisis of institutions, and a crisis of governance.

The power of digital media is, in many respects, the power of the small against the established. Audience power, as Tim Dunlop has written, has transformed the social contract underpinning the mainstream media, not least its habitually patronising, top-down attitudes to its users (Dunlop 2013). Its transformative effect on politics could be seen in the way that social media called out the mainstream media and put feminism back on newspaper front pages after Julia Gillard's speech on misogyny in 2012 was initially underestimated. Correctives to public missteps come fast in the world of social media, even as this same flexing of audience muscles, in many cases fuelled by low standards of evidence, provides fuel for opportunistic political populism and phenomena such as global warming denialism.

The global information ecology has fundamentally changed. And with it, the cultural centre of gravity is changing, and with that, the role of publishers has fundamentally changed. Knowledge has become plural – 'knowledges' – which are understood as culturally, even tribally, specific, and now come from below as much as from above. In the world of Facebook and Twitter, we more often put our faith in media networks of peers, not media institutions and expert knowledge. The traditional line between media producers and consumers, often overstated by enthusiasts of new media, has further blurred. Barriers to entry have fallen and ushered in a widely trumpeted age of the amateur (Leadbetter 2009; Shirky 2008). We famously live in an age of information excess, not scarcity. Increasingly, the primary task of publishers is no longer to bring a mediated flow of new information into the world, but to filter, curate, reframe and add value to already existing public information. Culture, in short, no longer comes primarily from above, from the restaurant lunch tables of publishers and the editor's desks of newspapers, or, indeed, the halls of Academe.

These changes have invited into our world far more complexity than is allowed by any battle between technophobes and techno-evangelists, which is how such changes have so often been figured, to the detriment of any real analysis. The present transformation isn't merely technological, it's political. It goes to the heart of the question of what type of world we want to live in. To understand the present transformation, we need to unpack the relationship between digital media and forms of political populism that advocate an all-pervasive, hard-edged free-market ideology; 'extreme capitalism', as Thomas Frank has called it (Frank 2001). Or 'supercapitalism', as Robert Reich has called the corporatism that has supplanted democratic capitalism (Reich 2008), leading to such things as widening income and wealth inequality, widespread employment insecurity, declining public infrastructure, and the domination of debates on such things as global warming by corporate interests. Political fearmongering that finds its strongest hold among those disenfranchised by economic reform is a central part of this package, which, promoted by an ascendant conservative move-ment, has begun to dictate terms to every traditional democratic form of understanding.

M. Patricia Marchak is probably the best historian of how the New Right were the first to understand the consequences of the technological revolution of the 1960s and 1970s, when the introduction of the transistor and the integrated circuit began to destabilise the traditional post-war economic order. Their response to the rise of Japan as a technological and economic force, in particular, involved a complex realignment of the economic and political norms of the post-World War II 'steel economy' to mobilise political forces to set in place a conservative, free-market agenda that would open up global markets to US products, deregulate the global economy so that US corporations could globalise supply chains and cut costs (not least in electronics manufacturing), and restructure and de-unionise the US economy around services, so as to restore US economic hegemony (Marchak 1993). Thomas Frank has since given an important account of how ideas about the relationship between the internet and democracy that emerged during the techno-euphoria of the dot-com boom of the early 2000s provided an archetype for what he calls 'market populism', whereby the market itself is considered the very definition of democracy; a reversal, as Frank points out, of the traditional idea that a primary function of democracy is to protect people from the worst excesses of markets (Frank 2001). Innovations such as Web 2.0 have since realised an almost complete integration of media plat-forms and markets.

Similarly, when we talk about the pressure for fast-track books, or the pressure to maximise shareholder value, what we talk about is a deeper social and political transformation: a shift from a social liberal conception of markets to one where public institutions and the public good have been pushed to one side by the imperatives of shareholder value and a corporatism obliged to seek profits in the first instance. What we are talking about, really, when we talk about the transformations in book publishing, is the deepening crisis of social liberalism and the public culture that went with it.

My question is: what kind of publishing will thrive in this new climate? What will its new big ideas be? What will its new literatures be? What will its values and aspirations be? What will the preoccupations of its long-form non-fiction be? What will its sources of knowledge be? The temptation for book publishers has been to search for a new digital business model. But what book publishing needs isn't simply a new business model. What book publishing needs is a new social model.

At base, publishing is a commercial enterprise founded on fostering human interconnectedness. Whether it be literary fiction, long-form current affairs, cookbooks, biographies, self-help or sport, publishing is about creating social commonalities. Reading is always a social act. Since the invention of moveable type printing by Gutenberg, which helped spark the Reformation and paved the way for the rise of science and the Enlightenment (Eisenstein 2012), and, more recently, the emergence of the modern public sphere, and, later still, the emergence of twentieth-century modernism and the liberation struggles of the second half of the twentieth century in such areas as feminism and indigenous rights, publishers have thrived when they are connected to social change.

So what might this new social model look like?

A hint of where new social models might come from can perhaps be heard in the Occupy movement, and in some of the more progressive political impulses seen during the Arab Spring. Or in environmental movements around climate change, or pro-democracy movements in Asia and the Middle East. Such movements, for all their differences and mixed successes, arguably have in common a desire to discover new forms of social settlement that move beyond the old Cold War divides that framed late twentieth-century debate: between collectivism versus individualism, and the culture wars between righteous conservatives and degenerate 'elites' that followed. There is something new brewing here. If digital networked culture has often helped propel such movements forward, then the question for publishers is: what kinds of voices will these movements bring forward to put sustained arguments in book-length form? How might publishers build an economy around such voices, and support them with income and time to think and write properly? If we are going to change the world – and we must, or these may literally become our environmental end times – then what will our communities of practice be, our guiding narratives, our coteries, our rituals and principles of organisation? And who will our leaders be, and our visionaries, and how might we give them voice in ways that reach across and glue together the various niches and byways of web-based electronic media?

What will come to replace old assumptions, if publishing is to continue to have a social function, is more than simply new channels. What we need is more prehensile, more imaginative ideas of what culture is and where it comes from. Of what progress means and how to achieve it. Ideas that can ignite and find resonance with readers looking for answers about their world. What we need, in short, is a new social contract. That is, a new way to connect democracy to cultural value, to citizenship, to returns for publishers and authors.

Already in the best publishing we see this: meaningful documentary accounts of the present. We see, too, online and in small publishers, the emergence of what might be called 'the new artisanship', which is where ideas are springing from. A few years ago I published some research on what I called 'the decline of the literary paradigm' in an increasingly market-led publishing culture, and speculated that literary publishing would become the preserve of enthusiasts (Davis 2007). Jan Zwar has recently identified how similar pressures have impacted on literary non-fiction publishing (Zwar 2012), with independent publishers taking on an important role in sustaining the genre. A shift has been taking place. A ground-up literary 'sub-politics' (Beck 1994) has begun to develop in small presses and small journals, and is developing new writers and winning prizes. If we leave aside the not-insignificant question of how small circulation titles might earn something of a living for authors and their publishers, this has turned out to not be such a bad thing. The new artisans of small presses and online media and small start-ups are increasingly custodians of culture, and are building new communities and new models, and, perhaps, new social contracts. They are demonstrating the use-value of book-length publishing and its connectedness to culture. Indeed, book publishing, if it's a business worth doing, *must* be at the centre of such projects. But the 'new publishing', if it can be called that, will be a publishing broadly defined, working across the range of channels and at the same time cognisant of and energised by its role in a broader social project.

If it might seem an odd thing to do to write about the challenges facing the book publishing industry and to end by calling for something of a social revolution, then that is precisely what I seek to do. Anything less would be to underestimate the connection between publishing and democratic society. For those of us who still believe in book-length publishing, in the special skills that long-form writers, publishers, editors, and marketers bring to democracy, and in the ability of that expertise to continually rewrite and renew democracy, questions about new business models, or the enthusiastic embrace of new channels, can only take us so far. We won't get anywhere if we don't reassess and reinvent the fundamental social reasons for *why* it is that publishers do what they do. This is because our questions about the future of the publishing industry turn out to be versions of our oldest questions. What kind of public sphere do we want, and what kind of social world do we want this to be?

Chapter 2

AT WAR WITH THE FUTURE

The Publishing Industry and the Digital Revolution

Peter Donoughue

The publishing industry, right now, is in a very funny place. We are in the throes of a digital transition that is radically challenging our traditional operations, structures, habits of mind and very identities. This is not news to anybody. My contention, however, is that we are seriously misdiagnosing this challenge, and adopting strategic postures to deal with it that are thoroughly wrong-headed. I want to start with a few observations about the Penguin Random House merger, as a lead-in to the central thrust of my argument. There's been a lot of very thoughtful stuff written about this merger, and I don't want to rehash that. I would say firstly though that, contrary to my claim above that we're wrong-headed about the way we're dealing with the digital challenge, this merger is absolutely right. It's the start of something good and necessary.

However, the experience of bedding down this combined operation is going to be terribly stressful and painful for the entire global staff of both Penguin and Random. They are in for a world of pain. This is what I wrote in a recent blog post:

> In my experience it is a far better outcome for everyone involved if companies are acquired rather than 'merged'. An acquisition means there is clarity around who is in charge, i.e. who sets the agenda and who has to give way; whose policies and processes take precedence; whose jobs will likely go. A merger means constant, ongoing political infighting at every level over things large and small.
>
> So many senior staff will be spending most of their time in meetings and conference calls 24/7, that is, internal navel-gazing, that the core objective of the business – competing in the fast changing marketplace

– will get far too little attention. The whole entity will suffer. This is so predictable and usually beyond the capability of management to prevent.

As well, morale generally hits rock-bottom. The people who win – who survive or get additional responsibilities – are universally the smooth and political, those who can best game the system. (Donoughue 2011)

Overlay onto this process the all-pervasive and negative effects of globalisation – the rationalisation of structures, systems, policies, processes and responsibilities across the globe – and you get a real and irreversible leaching of energy and competitive urgency from local, country-based operations like those in Australia. Australian subsidiary companies are very susceptible to this process: they are large enough to be respected, but not large enough to be critically important.

Henry Rosenbloom recently wrote in his blog that the Penguin Random merger was really nothing of the sort (2012). It was a takeover in all but name. I agree. What we're actually seeing is a slow-motion takeover of Penguin by Random House. And we will undoubtedly see more, most probably over the next year or so. HarperCollins will acquire Simon & Schuster or possibly Macmillan, and Hachette will acquire the other one. This is a logical and rational process, an inevitable outcome, because of what's driving it. Imagine for a moment the enormous advantages these mega-publishers will garner. They can afford to invest in very sophisticated software systems across all areas of the company including editorial, composition, production and distribution; they can contract cheaper printing; and squeeze suppliers of everything until their pips squeak. And they can even say to Amazon: 'Your ebook discount is now 30 per cent, not 50 per cent. Live with it.'

The industry, worldwide, is undergoing a massive revenue subsidence. Print revenues are shrinking (despite the uptick in the first nine months of 2012 mainly because of the *Fifty Shades of Grey* and *The Hunger Games* phenomena). United States print book sales fell 9.3 per cent in units in 2012 as a whole. Mass-market paperbacks, under assault from ebooks, fell 20.5 per cent, while trade paperbacks, according to Nielsen BookScan, 'fell more than hardbacks' (Cader 2013). In the United States in 2011 hardback revenues were down 17.5 per cent over 2010, and paperback revenues down 15.6 per cent. In the United Kingdom total print revenues were down 4.6 per cent in 2012, after declining 11 per cent in 2011. We don't have such precise figures in Australia but we all know anecdotally how depressing things generally are and how badly the collapse of REDgroup in 2011 hurt the industry. The very welcome strong growth of ebooks has ameliorated this situation – they now represent 26 per cent of total trade sales in the United States and a bit less in the United Kingdom – but the logic of lower-priced ebooks means more units but less revenues.

Thus the industry has no choice but to cut its traditional overheads by at least fifteen to 20 per cent to maintain profitability and continue to attract investor capital. The best way to do this is to radically cut duplication, and the best way to do that is for players to acquire, merge or partner. This is creative destruction at its best, and the book trade has seen it many times over the last 100 or so years. In the 1920s heavily discounted bestsellers began to be sold in non-traditional retail outlets like grocery and department stores; in the 1930s and 1940s book clubs subsequently emerged and prospered; by mid-century public libraries were rapidly spreading under new government funding initiatives, bringing free access to books to millions of patrons around the world; then the paperback was invented. Now it's the ebook revolution (Brown 2012). What is common to all these major disruptions? The offer of lower prices and vastly improved access, and the enthusiastic reader response.

We have our own rather significant circumstance in Australia – the dramatic strengthening of the Australian dollar over the last decade – which is putting downward pressure on prices. Australian publishers, distributors and others involved in importing have lowered prices by 10 to 15 per cent over the last few years under competitive pressure, but this is nowhere near enough. Prices should have been lowered by around 30 per cent to meet consumer expectations and to fend off Amazon, but of course this adds considerably to revenue decline unless there's a far more substantial – that is, around 50 per cent – increase in volume. And this requires not just a great deal of faith but a great deal of courage, and in our industry that's in short supply.

I was Managing Director of Wiley Australia in the early 2000s when the dollar started to climb, after five years or so of plumbing the depths, and the exhilaration in the company, shared by all importing businesses, at our increasing margins was palpable (and the executive bonuses bankable). But I soon realised it was wrong. I fought my own divisional managers fiercely to force them to lower prices regularly. We were the only company doing it. To me it was a matter of integrity as much as anything else – keeping faith with our customers, booksellers as well as readers. I've long argued that our booksellers' obsession with Amazon and its GST-free imports was misplaced. Of course we should welcome any move by the government to lower the $1000 threshold, but we're missing the real target. And that is massive over-pricing by Australian importing publishers that has gone on for far too long. We allowed Australian consumers to get hooked on Amazon and The Book Depository and the whole industry is now paying the price.

Now let me return to my main point. My contention is that the industry globally, apart from corporate rationalisation, is adopting strategic postures in the face of the digital challenge that are entirely misplaced. I want to talk about Google, then Amazon. And end with some optimism about the future.

We are all familiar with the Google Books Library Project. In 2004 Google began scanning, without seeking permission from authors and publishers, entire books that were held by half a dozen major university and public libraries in the United States and the United Kingdom. The purpose was not to sell the files subsequently but simply to offer snippets (two or three lines) around key terms entered by searchers, and then point them to where the book or file could be purchased or borrowed. About twelve million titles were eventually scanned before authors and publishers instituted legal action against Google. After a long period of negotiation, a complex settlement agreement was reached in 2009 and, according to proper legal process, presented to the United States Federal Court of Appeals for approval. It was rejected by the judge, unfortunately, principally because it gave Google a virtual monopoly, and thus the whole project was stopped in its tracks. In October 2012 the publishers came to a different sort of settlement with Google concerning works still on their lists – one that doesn't require court approval (Cader 2012) – but the authors, who are always very bolshie, are sticking to their litigation agenda.

Now here's the nub of the issue: Google always maintained that its scanning was 'fair use' under the terms of the United States *Copyright Act 1976*. After all, they were undertaking a scanning process that their library clients were already free to do under the law for archival purposes, they were not intending to offer the files for sale and were not impinging on a publisher's commercial terrain as there was no conceivable market for 'snippets' anyway. This always sounded to me as innocent an activity as cataloguing, shelving or browsing. It encourages discovery and eventual purchase by a consumer. What is more, the great majority of titles held in these major libraries were what are called 'orphan works': titles still in copyright but out of print where the original publisher and/or author could not be tracked or contacted. They were to be liberated: made discoverable and accessible to students, researches, hobbyists and readers. As a result of the litigation, those works are still rotting in the deep recesses of the world's libraries, unknown and unloved. Wouldn't it have been a wiser course for publishers and authors to welcome Google's scanning initiative and benefit from the sales of the discovered works that eventuated?

Now for another behemoth that's universally loathed and feared by the industry, to such an extent, it seems to me, as to have become quite pathological. I refer to Amazon. Now I'm not so naive as to defend everything Amazon has done and is still doing. It's a ruthless, aggressive operation that rides roughshod over its competition and more particularly over its suppliers. But I do want to lament the way the industry has dealt with Amazon since day one of the ebook take-off six years ago when the Kindle was first released. You all know the story. It's become the trade's standard, orthodox narrative.

Once upon a time Amazon invented an ebook reader and in a short space of time garnered nearly 90 per cent of the market for the new, revolutionary ebooks. Amazon demanded a 50 per cent discount off the ebook price of around $25.00 yet they priced the bestselling ebooks at $9.99, way below cost. The publishing community was aghast at this outrageous and cynical manoeuvre. 'This will lower price expectations across the board,' they lamented. 'It must be stopped.'

Fortunately a major new entrant appeared, called Apple, with its amazing iPad. It said to publishers, 'Use our app model – you set the price; we take 30 per cent commission as your agent. However you must not allow any other ebook retailer to undercut us on price.' The publishers rushed on board (whether after a boozy lunch at an up-market Manhattan establishment is a debatable point), and forced Amazon to adopt the agency model. This would end the discounting, they yelped, and restore order and security to the book world.

Well of course we know how the story then unfolded. The United States Department of Justice (DOJ) refused to believe the fairy tale and in April 2012 condemned Apple and the agency publishers for their collusion to restrict competition. It pronounced that the agency model had to be unwound.

The trade was aghast, and the condemnation of the DOJ has been universal. Last year respected industry consultant Mike Shatzkin opined, 'The legal experts applying their antitrust theories to the industry don't understand what they're monkeying with or what the consequences will be of what they see as their progressive thinking' (Shatzkin 2012). Shatzkin demands they respect the 'specialness' of the publishing ecosystem. By removing Amazon's ability to aggressively discount, the competitive landscape is enhanced. It allows other retailers to emerge and potentially flourish and not be crushed by a deep-pocket behemoth seeking dominance at all costs by indulging in 'predatory pricing'.

But I go back to my Economics 101 basics: it is not the prerogative of a producer to so constrict – for whatever reason – a retailer from engaging in the age-old dynamics of customer satisfaction. So no matter how large, voracious, aggressive, ugly, or profoundly discourteous any particular retailer is at any time, a producer just has to live with that retailer's consumer satisfaction strategy. Let's remember that, pre-agency, publishers were pricing their new ebooks at ludicrously high prices – often at the same price as the hardback – and in fact far higher than Apple demanded publishers price at if they wanted to deal with Apple. Ironically the consumer demand profile of recent times is unequivocally demonstrating that the greater volume of ebook sales occurs around the $10 mark, and falls off quite rapidly at price points beyond that.

Now, post the DOJ decision, the fear of many is that Amazon will return not just with renewed vigour, but also with a good measure of vengeance. Some commentators are indulging in truly awful effusions of doom and apocalypse, booksellers in particular, who for a variety of reasons have no reason to love this online enemy (Copyright Agency, 2012). But the agency model, like any price-fixing model, is a dead hand. My view is that if in the end we all trade in an open, unconstrained, free market then it is not naive to believe that we will all be better off in the long run. New, original, highly innovative business models will have a far higher chance of emerging if the dead hands of tradition, authority, stability and comfort are not privileged. Protective shells need to be broken to allow new life to emerge.

The industry went to war with Google; it's still at war with Amazon; it's at war with the United States Department of Justice. Publishers are at war with authors over ebook royalties; they are at war with libraries over ebook lending; even with consumers over digital rights management (DRM) (Doctorow 2012). All these wars are shameful. But what really amazes me is how we have sniffily turned our backs on what has clearly been the greatest financial investment in books and reading ever seen. Billions of dollars have been spent over the last decade alone in building a whole new digital ecosystem to take our content to millions of existing and, particularly, new readers around the world. Think of the enormous investment that Google has made into reaching into the content of virtually every book published since Gutenberg and making it discoverable and accessible to the entire world's population. This could only be of benefit to publishers. Think of the hundreds of millions of dollars Amazon, Apple, Kobo, Sony, Nook and others have made in bringing ereading technology to the world's consumers. It's a massive reach out to the non-traditional, non-bookshop-visiting consumer, particularly the young who can now be distracted from HBO, Showcase and BitTorrent, and can access content we publish on their must-have devices, including their smart phones.

Why haven't we embraced, in fact, celebrated this? Why have we been struck by a paralysing timidity; an awful defensiveness; a demobilising moral panic; a reactionary urge to protect our dated, legacy business models; a tentativeness that borders on the absurd? Why haven't we begun working positively with these behemoths to secure win-win outcomes of real benefit to consumers, and equal benefit to publishers by eliminating DRM, closed systems, restrictive licensing arrangements, et cetera?

Here's where small and medium independent publishers can and should take the lead. They are a dynamic and vibrant sector, the hope of the future. They don't have to worry about savagely cutting costs; they don't have any to begin with. They are not captive to a corporate line, a groupthink. They don't lack courage – they've chosen to be in publishing after all. They don't have to adopt the conservative, timid, strategic postures of the corporates. They can have a go, take risks, experiment. And their opportunity to thrive will grow stronger as the big publishers turn inwards and, under financial pressure, think only big. Ever more gems will be considered small beer by them – distractions from their core business. But these works are just as necessary to our cultural and social development as they ever were.

Chapter 3

WHAT NEXT FOR THE AUSTRALIAN BOOK TRADE?

Tim Coronel

When I first worked behind the counter of a chain bookshop in a suburban Canberra shopping mall in 1990, there were two cash registers, one telephone, a microfiche reader for Books In Print and, in the back room, the latest tech: a fax machine. We memorised the stock on hand, and would do stock checks and write up reorders by hand on carbon pads, faxing them to publishers and distributors, where a small army of 'customer service' employees would be keying the orders into green-screen computers. While there was a head office and some central buys of major titles, the store manager spent much of her week seeing publishers' sales reps, and she had autonomy on ordering most of the stock for the shop.

In the ensuing twentyish years, many things have changed drastically, but, other than a few hiccups – such as the introduction of the GST in 2000 and the collapse of Collins Booksellers in 2005 (quickly reborn, phoenix-like, as a successful franchise network) – the Australian book industry developed, matured and grew steadily in the 1990s and 2000s. Not that selling books has ever been that profitable – publishing is gambling writ large, and the returns are modest: single-figure net profits and market growth are thought of as 'good', but if they are viewed as compounding over twenty years, then the trade certainly has grown.

A quick aside: I'll be talking here of the mainstream, 'trade' side of the book industry – essentially 'reading for pleasure' commercial publishing and the retail business that sells its products. Before we even think of 'publishing' more widely, reaching into newspapers, magazines, online, and so on, 'book publishing' as an industry is almost half educational publishing, from primary school materials to high school textbooks, tertiary texts and professional journals. This is a large and important part of the industry, but one that is largely beyond my remit.

One of the main catalysts for the development of the Australian book industry was the *Copyright Amendment Act 1991*, which enshrined the parallel import restrictions that have been in contention so often since. By creating a solid, protected market for local editions of overseas-originated books, a 'portfolio' model became the norm for Australian publishing companies. Both locally-owned, independent publishers – such as Allen & Unwin, Text, Scribe, Black Inc., Hardie Grant and many others – and the local branches of the big international publishers – Penguin, Random House, HarperCollins, PanMacmillan, Hachette and Simon & Schuster – developed businesses that combined 'buy-ins' of overseas-originated titles with their publication of local books. And as these companies grew, they were better equipped to participate in international rights markets at events such as the Frankfurt, London and Bologna book fairs, and to sell rights to Australian books to many other territories. (There is a downside to this model, however. It is estimated that many of the larger companies are reliant on sales of overseas-derived titles for up to 55 per cent of their revenue. If, as we will get to shortly, a growing proportion of Australian readers are buying these books online and offshore, then a crucial part of Australian publishers' business model is being eroded.)

Bookselling was pretty healthy as well through the 1990s and 2000s. Independent bookshops maintained a substantial market share, chain stores served the mass-market well, and the massive discounting wars that distorted the United Kingdom and United States book trades and moved much of bookselling there into supermarkets and discount mass retailers were largely averted.

But then, a few years ago, something happened – or, rather, a few 'somethings' coincided. It wasn't sudden, and to be honest, we'd all known it was coming, but we still weren't prepared for its impact.

Amazon started selling books online in 1995, and other online booksellers, local and global, followed. The momentum took a while to build among the general public, but before long it was easy to look up any book online and do price comparisons. It was no longer an automatic choice to buy books at your local bricks-and-mortar bookshop. But, much of the time, even if an individual title seemed much cheaper overseas, exchange rates and shipping costs meant that it wasn't all that much cheaper by the time it got to your door.

But once the Australian dollar got to parity with the US, and then some, and stayed there (and got to 60 pence against the British Pound), the massive scale and loss-leading discounting of Amazon and The Book Depository (which was bought by Amazon in 2011) meant that the sort of book that was $30 in your local bookshop (and which frequently really needs to be $30, or close to that, to cover its costs – but that's a detailed argument for another time) could be had, at your door in a matter of days, for half that.

Ebooks also were a slow-burner, and have been talked about since the 1990s. But until the rise of the Amazon Kindle and similar inexpensive, always-online hand-held ereader devices, there wasn't much of a commercial argument for them. But, again, the speed of take-up of ebooks since 2007 has been phenomenal. Amazon jumped in and dominated the ebook and ereader device markets with Kindle, and drove the perception that ebooks should cost US$9.99, or even less. (And remember: while Dymocks tried to start selling ebooks in 2007, Australians only got access to the Kindle store in late 2009, to Kobo in May 2010, to Apple iBooks and Google Ebooks both in November 2010, and to local start-up Booki.sh in January 2011. This is all very recent.) In Australia, ebooks currently comprise about 10 per cent of publishers' revenues, but in the US, they now make up at least a quarter of mainstream publishers' revenues, and there are many titles, especially in genre and popular fiction, that are ebook-dominant or ebook-only. The proportion of books sold as ebooks will continue to grow. Will it plateau? We don't know.

The 2011 collapse of REDgroup, the private equity-funded owner of Borders and Angus & Robertson, wasn't directly due to online competition or ebooks. The business model and culture of REDgroup was really at fault. But the aftermath has been very instructive. REDgroup's market share – at least a high-teens proportion of mainstream Australian book sales – just hasn't been replaced. That proportion of the retail market was already gone – gone online and offshore. Local publishers are suffering, of course, and many have reported that their sales are down 20 per cent or more.

I'm going to move away now from the historical explication and get dot-pointy with some assertions and predictions about where things are headed. It's important to note that all the following assertions are 'and', not 'or', statements. There will be print books *and* ebooks. There will be large publishers *and* small ones. There will be bookshops on our streets *and* there will be online sellers delivering to our doors or to our devices. There will be authors who do exceedingly well by self-publishing and handling their own affairs, *and* there will be authors who will benefit from having a traditional publisher back them. But what is clear is that the established ways of doing business in book-world have changed forever.

Assertions

- 'Book culture' in Australia is currently very healthy: there are writers' festivals all over the country that draw crowds into the tens of thousands; most nights in most cities you will find a book launch or author event being held at a local bookshop; children's authors are out and about in schools and libraries; literary magazines are going gangbusters; and genres such as romance and sci-fi/fantasy, with their passionate fans, are holding more and more, and bigger and bigger events.

- Australians currently read as much as ever, but their buying patterns have changed dramatically already and will continue to change.

- Nielsen BookScan's pie showing one-third market share each for independent bookshops, chain stores and discount department stores (such as Target and Big W) doesn't include local online sellers, let alone overseas ones, and doesn't measure ebook sales. The pie is more likely split five ways. Amazon and The Book Depository combined (now under common ownership, remember) have almost as much market share as any local sector, and are worth hundreds of millions of dollars. This is where the 'missing twenty per cent' from the local market has gone. Their share will continue to grow, and we won't get it back. More and more of the bestselling titles will be bought online, as ebooks or in print, and many consumers' default online choices are offshore. We are now dealing not just with Amazon but also with Apple and Google and Sony: the global book industry is utterly tiny in comparison to these behemoths.

- While 'book culture' in Australia is very healthy (and diverse, not just literary), there are no real signs that the pool of readers is increasing, and it may well shrink as baby boomers die off and the next generation's reading and consumption habits change. While there is a lot of book buzz, is it all preaching to the converted? What can the trade do to increase the number of book readers?

Predictions

- The 1991 parallel import legislation will be dead with the next change of government, but that might not even be necessary by then. Readers are doing their own importing, and publishers have been forced to move closer to simultaneous release for many titles (although is fourteen days any better than 30 in a 'want it now' online world?)

- Global English-language rights will become more and more prevalent, as will simultaneous worldwide publishing. Where this leaves author tours, writers' festivals and associated marketing, which until now has been staggered with territory-by-territory release dates, is a key problem.

- (Near-)parity pricing will be essential, even if it seems commercially suicidal, and will need to move quickly with currency fluctuations.

- The local offices of global publishers have already contracted, and will continue to have to 'rationalise' and restructure as the market shifts. One or more may leave this market altogether, or even cease to exist globally. The 'Random Penguins' will likely be the first of a number of mergers: will it be Harper & Schuster next? Almost all the biggest trade companies are part of diversified international cross-media businesses – will these companies (News Corp, Viacom, Lagardere, et al.) continue to see value in owning a book-publishing arm?

- It's possible that one or more of the well-known Australian independent publishers won't be able to weather the changes and will have to close or merge. We've already seen Murdoch Books taken over by Allen & Unwin.

- More bookshops will close, I suspect in suburban high streets and regional towns next, both indies and franchise-owned chain stores. However, existing inner-city stores, mainly indies, will prosper if they continue to be smart and proactive with their connections to reader communities.

- Among the online-only retailers, will there be more diversity, or will Amazon eventually steamroll everyone? (And/or will diversity be driven by niche, online genre specialists and 'social reading' sites that hook into communities but utilise affiliate revenue, rather than being 'retailers' per se?)

- 'Showrooming' may well be legitimised, with publishers paying for (even more) display space in prominent stores, yet content to see customers buying online.

- Book distribution will need to shrink, physically, yet improve service levels and tech smarts dramatically. In Australia, we can't maintain all these 'sheds' owned by individual publishers. Macmillan is the first of the distributors to announce the wind-up of its distribution service (However, smaller independent publishers are reliant on this third-party distribution to get their books into stores and into readers' hands.)

- A consolidated distributor (maybe a local branch of US-based Baker & Taylor or Ingram) will emerge (although it might be offshore, in New Zealand or South-East Asia).

- Prizes as publishing (aka the Vogel model) will become even more common; advances (and even royalty income) will be much less of a sure thing for authors. Getting a second and subsequent book published will be harder and harder; the semi-career of being a mid-list author is in severe danger.

- 'Worthy' publishing will be even more subsidy-reliant, but, as reaction to the recent Book Industry Strategy Group report has shown, the book trade will have a hard time convincing governments to give more funding. Mooted changes to the way the Australia Council's Literature Board hands out funding may well enshrine a number of subsidised publishers as 'the keepers of Oz lit'.

- In many cases, Australian publishers will have to accept more of an 'incubator' role for local authors, and be prepared to lose authors to big international players.

- Australian publishers will increasingly need to base their lists on titles for local consumption and learn to live without many sales of overseas-originated books.

Accentuate the Positives: It's Not All Doom and Gloom

- The local industry will be more 'Australian', with less of its energies focused on promoting the overseas-originated titles that have been their bread and butter.

- Authors/books with obvious global potential will get there, and probably quicker.

- Literary magazines (in print and online) and small publishers are flourishing and will become even more important, as incubators and as the home for adventurous publishing (they also have less of a financial imperative – passion over profit).

- There will be more use of agile technology: ebooks, apps, print on demand. Books will be made successful by appealing directly to communities of readers online, and less so to mainstream media.

But …

Where's the money? What sized local industry will be financially viable? I suspect it will be considerably smaller than what we have now. What will happen to skills? Will authors, and freelance/part-time bookmakers, be able to afford to continue? If we lose even moderate economies of scale, will local books be even more expensive to produce and even less likely to return a profit?

Chapter 4

UNINTENDED CONSEQUENCES

The Impact of Structural Reform in the Newspaper Industry on
the Marketing of Books

Sybil Nolan and Matthew Ricketson

This study considers recent changes to Australia's major newspapers, and their unintended consequences for book publishing. Around 2008–09, the Australian newspaper industry suffered a serious reversal. Revenues dropped dramatically: by more than 10 per cent, according to industry analyst IBISWorld (Fitzpatrick 2012, 4–5). While the end of the global financial crisis resulted in a partial restoration of newspapers' fortunes as business confidence recovered, another development threatened the industry. The advent of smart phones and tablets, which coincided with the economic downturn, saw large numbers of readers migrating online for news and information, further intensifying pressure on the newspaper business model (ibid.; Australian Communications and Media Authority 2013). The major newspaper companies, News Limited and Fairfax, both responded by slashing staff, streamlining internal operations and reducing pagination.[1] Their newspapers' literary coverage was not immune to these changes, which came at a time when booksellers were undergoing one of the toughest trading periods in recent memory.[2] This article examines the structural reforms in the News Ltd. and Fairfax press, focusing particularly on the Saturday books sections of the Fairfax dailies, to shed insight on their impacts on the book industry.

---

[1]   News Ltd. was renamed News Corp Australia in July 2013.

[2]   *Australian Bookseller and Publisher* described 2012 as 'one of the toughest years in the trade in a long time' (2012). Also, 'Nielsen BookScan figures: overall sales down, top 10 up' (2012).

The Trouble with Newspapers

In Australia, the book and newspaper industries have been interdependent since the colonial era. Books – generally speaking, books were published in Britain – provided the colonial press with a rich source of content (often gratis). In turn, this content provided a source of free publicity for books and authors. Local journalists' summaries of new releases were a reliable way of filling newspaper column inches, providing a link with important literary developments at 'home' and a focus for the incipient Australian publishing industry while enriching humdrum parochial coverage. By the 1880s, weekly installments from serialised novels and biographies were a 'major source of entertainment' in *The Sydney Morning Herald*, *The Australasian*, *The Age* and other leading newspapers (Morrison 1988; Morrison 1998). As Elizabeth Morrison noted, the press was the dominant force in Australian print culture in the colonial era (ibid.). Visitors from overseas noted, often with a degree of surprise, that the quality of literary coverage in the Australian press was generally reliable, and sometimes much better than that; the tenor of this commentary carried over to the twentieth century.[3]

In 1971, John Colmer, a British academic and literary critic who became a fixture at the University of Adelaide, observed, in a survey of press reviewing in this country:

> When I first arrived in Australia ten years ago I was puzzled by the embarrassed silence that followed my attempts to discuss any book reviews I had recently read. Then one day it was made quite clear to me that I had been guilty of an unAustralian activity and that the sooner I confined my conversation to essentials the better, essentials being staff-student ratios and the minutiae of Departmental administration. It was a heart-chilling experience from which I have never quite recovered, but perhaps my experience was unrepresentative. Certainly, in 1971, the evidence suggests that more and more people are taking an interest in books and book reviewing: more space is given to books in the newspapers than ten years ago; the standard of reviewing is higher; and there has been a great improvement in format and presentation. (Colmer 1971, 344)

Australians, all being 'good Benthams' at heart, showed 'more interest in pingpong diplomacy than Black Mountain poets' (ibid.), Colmer thought, and this was reflected in the review sections' interest in international affairs,

---

[3]   See for example the American journalist and scholar, Holden (1961): 'Australian book reviewing is of good quality – sometimes of superlative'.

politics and sport over fiction. Nor were there enough specialists commissioned to write reviews, except perhaps in *The Canberra Times*. Nonetheless, he concluded that many of the metropolitan dailies maintained 'far higher standards of reviewing than the mass circulation dailies in England, and certainly *The Australian*, at least, compares favourably with the English *Guardian*' (ibid.).

By the time of Colmer's article, the interdependency between the press and publishing in Australia had developed a settled character, becoming a major plank of publishers' and booksellers' marketing strategies, just as it was in other great newspaper cultures. As book publishing became more concentrated, and large conglomerates began to dominate the industry globally in the 1970s and 1980s, marketing became even more central to its activities (Guthrie 2011, 12; Galligan 2007, 41–43).[4] By corollary, the book industry's appetite for free press publicity grew. As small independent publishers sprang up, they joined the list of houses crowding the desks of literary editors with review titles.

Using press publicity to sell books worked well enough when newspapers were fat in the 70s, 80s and late 90s. In those years, papers like *The Sydney Morning Herald*, *The Age*, *The Herald*, *The Australian*, and the *Australian Financial Review* expanded their scope for features dramatically, publishing lifestyle sections and inserted magazines which grew more lavish as technology improved. Behind this astonishing outpouring of quality colour inserts, circulation studies showed that the Western press continued its long-term decline (Goot 1979; Stephens 1997, 288). The twenty-first century presented newspapers with further profound challenges: the so-called 'great recession' and the arrival of Web 2.0, the second phase of wired communication, in which leading online stakeholders strategically repositioned the Web 'as platform' – that is, as a source of services rather than a media site in itself (Allen 2012; O'Reilly 2005).

In Australia, symptoms of mainstream media strain began to show themselves. In January 2008, *The Bulletin*, which had played a historic role in promoting the idea of a national literature, was made defunct. Subsequently, the local editions of *Time* and *Newsweek* folded. In late 2011, the *Australian Literary Review* lost its funding and was shut down by its publisher, *The Australian* newspaper. A few well-made lifestyle supplements, such as *The Sydney Morning Herald*'s Essential Style, quietly disappeared.

---

4   Mark Davis dates the impact in Australia of conglomeration slightly later, from the mid-1990s (2006, 93).

The British literary journalist William Skidelsky highlighted the vulner-ability of literary coverage as the viability of the traditional press came into question:

> The old financial model of newspapers is looking increasingly unsus-tainable, and this makes it inevitable that editors and proprietors will start questioning – if they haven't done already – the worth of book reviews. What is their purpose? What value do they add? (Skidelsky 2008, 35)

Notable American newspapers had long since rationalised their books coverage and cut review space (Hoffert 2010). Nevertheless, for an extended period the Australian literary sections held up their end. *The Weekend Australian's* Review section gradually grew in pagination between 2000 and 2010. *The Age* was able to devote marginally more space to books, by late 2008 running nine pages of books in its A2 section on Saturdays. *The Canberra Times* for many years ran at least eight pages of books coverage in its weekly Panorama section.[5]

The minerals boom kept the domestic economy relatively strong, and the newspaper industry's revenue streams were relatively protected. Yet, with hindsight, it is clear that the Australian newspaper business model hit the wall sometime around 2008, as the global financial crisis made itself felt and, coincidentally, smart phones and tablets became available to Australian consumers. Growth in GDP per capita peaked in 2007, then fell heavily, and measures of business confidence plunged at the same time (Australian Bureau of Statistics 2012; Fitzpatrick, 3). While both recovered quickly, their sudden decline exacerbated the long-term trend of newspaper industry decline (Fitzpatrick, 7). At almost the same moment, the iPhone was released in Australia, followed by other smart phones and the iPad. In the space of a single year, the number of mobile internet subscribers grew from just over eighteen million to 22 million (Australian Communications and Media Authority, 2). By May 2012, more than 80 per cent of the nation's nine million smart phone users accessed news, sport and weather updates online (ibid.). These changes had further consequences for newspaper advertising revenue, as advertisers also migrated to the Web (Ryan, 225; Allday, 2013).

Faced with a crisis in their traditional business model, news organisations responded by cutting underperforming newspaper sections, reducing staff, tightening contributor budgets and streamlining internal processes to share

---

[5]   *The Canberra Times* was owned by Fairfax from the 1960s until the late 1980s. In the period under study it was owned first by John B. Fairfax's Rural Press group, then by Fairfax Media from 2007.

more copy and editorial staff. News Ltd. moved to seven-day operations at several of its mastheads, reducing duplication of feature and review coverage in weekday and Sunday papers. Across its major morning tabloids in Adelaide, Melbourne, Sydney and Brisbane, there was far-reaching standardisation of lifestyle and personal finance sections. Fairfax also increased sharing of copy between sections, explaining to investors that it was 'optimising' its metropolitan newspapers for the online era to 'provide flexibility to move the business to a digital-only model', if that was what was necessary in future (quoted in Fitzpatrick, 29).

This standardisation and copy-sharing had direct impacts on lifestyle sections that were a significant part of book publishers' marketing models. In News Ltd.'s morning tabloids, Taste (food) and Your Money (personal finance) exemplified the high degree of uniformity the company had evolved in this sort of content across its national group (uniformity which would not necessarily be evident to readers dipping into their hometown morning papers). Both these sections were also associated with high-profile websites: taste.com.au and yourmoney.com.au. This integration of newspaper and web content was driven through NewsLifeMedia, a division formerly known as News Magazines, but now the hub of integrated publishing across News Ltd.'s various platforms (*Mumbrella* 2012; www.taste.com.au 2010). Fairfax Media, which had a tradition of editorial independence among its individual mastheads, also pushed back against longstanding staff resistance to copy-sharing, pursuing a policy of sharing stories and reviews and coordinating commissioning by similar sections.

The Impact on Book Marketing

The centralisation and rationalisation of commissioning had an impact on trade publishers with significant lifestyle lists – for example, food and wine lists and travel and personal finance imprints. There were fewer opportunities for, say, cookbook authors to write for Epicure or Taste, or for an extract of their latest book to run. As the marketing director of one medium-sized publisher commented, 'The new system is all or nothing: fantastic if you get in all of them, but not if you miss out' (Ryan 2012).

The copy-sharing strategy also had direct impacts on the Saturday book sections of Fairfax's morning papers in Melbourne, Sydney and Canberra. As the accompanying table shows, the majority of book reviews which appeared in Saturday's *Age*, *The Sydney Morning Herald* and *The Canberra Times* in a key period in 2012 were items shared between the papers; through sharing, a mere nineteen articles accounted for a majority of the 77 articles published. Perhaps surprisingly, given Melbourne's perennial fear of being overshadowed by Sydney, the *Sydney Morning Herald*'s books pages suffered more than *The Age*'s, hit not only by copy-sharing, but also by deep cuts to the number of books pages.

Comparing the Books Pages

Number of pages devoted to books				
	27 Oct 2012	3 Nov 2012	10 Nov 2012	Total
Age	9	8	8	25
Canberra Times	6	8	7	21
Sydney Morning Herald	6	6	7	19
Weekend Australian	8	8	8	24

Number of reviews published each week				
	27 Oct 2012	3 Nov 2012	10 Nov 2012	Total
Age	10	9	10	29
Canberra Times	8	11	9	28
Sydney Morning Herald	5	7	8	20

Note: Interviews with writers are included in the count for this table but not by-lined columns written by literary editors or contributors. There are four short reviews of fiction books and four short reviews of non-fiction books published weekly. In all the tables these short reviews are counted as one.

Uniformity of reviews				
Uniformity of reviews	27 Oct 2012	3 Nov 2012	10 Nov 2012	TOTAL
Reviews duplicated in all three Fairfax newspapers	4	4	1	27
Reviews duplicated in two of the three Fairfax papers	2	3	5	20
Number of reviews found in only one of the three papers	7	9	14	30

Number of books reviewed in only one of three newspapers, broken down by newspaper				
	27 Oct 2012	3 Nov 2012	10 Nov 2012	TOTAL
Age	4	3	4	11
Canberra Times	3	6	8	17
Sydney Morning Herald	0	0	2	2

Prepared by Matthew Ricketson, December 2012.

The *Sydney Morning Herald*'s literary editor, Susan Wyndham, confirmed that her section ran at between six and ten pages until, in the first half of 2012, the number was cut to six or seven (Wyndham 2012). She was told that the reduction was based on the decline in advertising revenue across the paper, economies in print and production costs, and the reduction in editorial staff. This explains why, on the last Saturday of October and the first Saturday of November 2012, in the busiest period of the year for book releases, *The Sydney Morning Herald* did not publish a single review that was exclusive to its pages. Wyndham said it was 'an absolute rule' (ibid.) that there should be as little duplication as possible of the sister review sections' commissioning, with the result that almost all the reviews she ran were shared. She was concerned about the impact of this for books and authors:

> I'm very disappointed by all this. I absolutely understand the company's financial imperatives, but as a literary editor I believe it is very important for the culture that the newspaper carries a diversity of voices, both for readers and for authors. What if the three newspapers carry the one negative review of a book? That would mean too much weight being given to one view. In their own way, the diversity of literary and cultural ideas is as important as the diversity of political ideas on the opinion pages. (ibid.)

The Age and *The Canberra Times*, which retained more pages, managed to run more reviews that were specific to their publication or shared with only one other paper. But for *The Canberra Times*, this outcome was guaranteed after a backlash by readers over plans to scale down its coverage.

In August 2012, its literary editor's position was made redundant. Gia Metherell, who had held the post since 2004, had been informed by her employers that in future *The Canberra Times* would carry the same books pages as *The Age* and *The Sydney Morning Herald*. According to Metherell, Fairfax Media's Metro editorial director, Garry Linnell, told her: 'Why should we pay three times for reviews of the same book?' (Linnell 2012).[6]

When word got out about Fairfax's plans, which also would have affected the paper's arts coverage, there was a fierce response from Canberra's cultural community. This caused Fairfax's management to reconsider, promising that

---

[6]   Interviewed for this article, Linnell did not remember saying this to Metherell, but agreed with the sentiment.

two or three locally sourced reviews would continue to appear each week, commissioned by the paper's editor. On the figures gathered for this article, it appeared that, as at early December 2012, the paper's literary pages had held up better than many Canberrans feared. The paper still had at least as much space for reviews as its Sydney and Melbourne sisters, and still ran more one-off reviews (many more, sometimes). Nevertheless, in some weeks it carried four or five reviews sourced from the other papers. Metherell commented: 'In my time as literary editor *The Canberra Times* would have reviewed just about every Australian debut author of any serious intent. What we have now is fewer voices examining fewer other voices (ibid.).' *The Age*'s literary editor, Jason Steger, also expressed concern that 'we do not have as many critical voices as we used to' (Steger 2012).

As John Colmer's long-ago colleague might have asked, what does this matter? Do book reviews in the Saturday newspapers even have an impact? The value of a review to book sales is difficult to determine empirically. Many researchers have tried, counting articles and comparing the counts with actual book purchases. An influential American survey of several such studies looked at the evidence regarding purchases by libraries. It found that for adult trade titles, there was a clear relationship between the number of reviews a title received and the likelihood that it would be acquired by a library. It was of little consequence whether the review was positive or negative (Blake 1989, 1–2). In a recent count-and-compare test, the American trade bible, *Publishers Weekly*, used BookScan data to look at bookshop sales of non-fiction releases after they had been noticed in the *New York Times Book Review*. It suggested that, while a bad review in an influential publication could finish a book, word of mouth and the zeitgeist were as critical as a good review (*Publishers Weekly* 2012, 8–9).

This fits with the accepted wisdom: that reviews 'help a book's sale chances, but even exceptionally positive reviews … cannot guarantee success in what is an exceedingly crowded market' (Greco, Rodriguez and Wharton 2007, 51). Yet, at the same time the Fairfax press was rationalising their book coverage in response to the economic downturn and fundamental changes in media, the book industry was experiencing similar pressures, and needed any helping hand it could get. Nielsen BookScan data showed that, in 2012, sales through Australian bookstores dropped 9.3 per cent in value. As industry observer Tim Coronel noted, the last good year was 2009, when book sales increased by a modest 5 per cent. Since then, they had 'fallen off a cliff' (Coronel 2012). Increasingly, big names like Jamie Oliver and Bryce Courtenay (not to mention print editions of the ubiquitous E. L. James) dominated the bestseller lists by a long way, and the spread of sales among other titles published in the peak pre-Christmas period in 2012 was not as strong as publishers had hoped. As Coronel pointed out, the industry has had to revise downwards its estimate of what a bestseller that is not a 'killer title' can achieve.

The specific factors that contributed to the adverse climate for bookselling after 2010 included the relentless rise of ereaders, the challenges posed by Amazon's dominance in the marketplace, and the public's sudden love affair with self-published ebooks such as James's *Fifty Shades of Grey*. As well, the book industry was still suffering the effects of the closure of the Borders and Angus & Robertson bookstore chains in 2011, which left publishers struggling to find retailers for their usual print runs. In such an environment, publishers were unlikely to lightly forgo reviews in the mainstream press, which was particularly true both for small- and medium-sized publishers with modest budgets for advertising, or no budgets at all, and for less popular titles.

For trade non-fiction – particularly books about issues of the moment, and celebrity biography or memoir – radio and television publicity is often more crucial than reviews in achieving sales momentum. But fiction is a different matter, particularly literary fiction, which depends on the oxygen of the books pages more than any other form except poetry. Mark Davis has described the phenomenon he dubbed 'the decline of the literary paradigm' – that is, the recent transition from an Australian publishing culture committed to creating a national literature to one focused on 'picking winners' (Davis, 94). Trade publishers have reduced their publishing of literary fiction and first-time authors. Reviews are vital to the marketing of such titles that still achieve publication, and a review in the Fairfax press is highly desirable. For a new or little-known author, such notice not only introduces them to a potentially large audience, but also helps create for them an enduring public profile, because the review becomes part of the digital archive available online.

Moreover, published reviews of first-time authors are more likely to be positive, particularly where fiction is concerned. Literary editors are interested in unearthing new talent for their readerships: there is little point dedicating space to negative reviews of books by writers no one has heard of. Such reviews are a vital legitimation of emerging writers and their works. Publishers seize on them, publicising them on Twitter and on their company websites, integrating them into press releases, and – if a reprint eventuates – running excerpts as cover lines. While publishers increasingly use social media to build strong communities of readers interested in genre fiction (romance, erotica, sci-fi, fantasy), they acknowledge the significance of the books pages to literary fiction: 'broadsheet reviews for us are the most important' (Swinn, 2012). For the sorts of titles that win prestigious prizes, traditional newspapers' combination of credibility and reach still matters, despite the growing number of dedicated literary bloggers and tweeters and sites such as Goodreads. As a senior publisher at one of Australia's largest trade publishing houses said:

> It doesn't tend to be literary fiction that goes viral on social media. Quiet domestic drama is not going to create the viral impetus in the way a work of Zombie erotica will. But generally speaking, when a literary title like Anna Funder's *All That I Am* has already reached a critical mass of readers, it's then that social media can help sell more copies of it. (Gilliatt 2012)

It is not only literary fiction by new authors that stands to lose when books pages are reduced and fewer reviews are published. Specialist and scholarly non-fiction are also affected. *The Canberra Times*, with its resident audience of policymakers, academics and technicians, has made such titles a mainstay of its literary pages over the years. Its traditional concern with national policy reached into corners of Australian life and public administration often ignored by the Sydney and Melbourne presses. Its Panorama supplement has been the go-to review section for savvy publishers struggling to achieve coverage of titles about serious issues or biographies of lesser-known but still significant lives. The changes to Fairfax's books coverage meant that there was no guarantee this would continue. For readers with old-fashioned newspaper habits, the *Canberra Times*'s books pages have been all the more memorable for the joy of the unexpected find. 'The best place to live for reading reviews is clearly Canberra,' John Colmer opined in 1971, and, until recently, the same could still have been argued, not only because of the *Canberra Times*' coverage, but also because of the easy access to a wealth of alternative coverage in *The Sydney Morning Herald* and *The Age*.

The Future

The picture painted by this article is, generally speaking, one of declining books coverage in the major Australian daily press. Both major newspaper groups, as they battled structural challenges to their industry, had restricted the opportunities available to book publicists by consolidating their lifestyle sections and moving to shared commissioning. In relation to book reviews, the *Sydney Morning Herald*'s literary coverage showed severe impacts of editorial cutbacks; *The Canberra Times* had lost a dedicated literary editor; and the majority of reviews across Fairfax's three city dailies were shared.

Yet the picture of reviewing in the mainstream press was not all gloomy. *The Weekend Australian* gave no sign, in late 2012, when this article was researched, that it planned any further reduction of its literary reportage and reviewing. Some of the morning tabloids, notably the *Herald Sun*, had ramped up their books coverage significantly.

The elephant in the room was e-publishing. At the time of writing, none of the mainstream papers had yet begun to review ebooks in a systematic way, even though, by then, trade publishers said that between 5 and 25 per cent of their adult fiction sales were of ebooks. In late 2012, IBISWorld noted predictions that ebooks could account for up to 50 per cent of all books sold in the next decade. It commented: 'The ramifications of such predictions are significant and will create immense changes for the book market and the way it is served (Fitzpatrick, 8).'

Although the growth in ebook sales flattened out significantly in the first half of 2013, there seems little reason to doubt the centrality of ebooks to fiction's future (Abrams, 2013). How these titles will be marketed is a subject ripe for further analysis. The emerging model is primarily a social media model: 'blog tours' for authors, author and publisher Twitter accounts and Instagram activity. It is conceived outside traditional media, and often bypasses it almost completely, partly because of the review sections' limited interest. If literary editors of traditional review sections continue to treat e-publishing as non-mainstream publishing, and to give it little oxygen except when it achieves the phenomenal success of a *Fifty Shades of Grey*, the historic interdependency of the press and book publishing will probably unravel further, with consequences for the national conversation about books and ideas.

II. Small Press Publishing

Chapter 5

DON'T LOOK BACK

Contemporary Independent Magazine Publishing beyond the Digital Divide

Caroline Hamilton

I have spent the past several years examining the kinds of social and intellectual changes that digital communications are bringing about in Australia's small publishing sector. These changes encompass many of the instrumental aspects of doing business as a small publisher from layout, design and distribution to publicity, fundraising and content creation.[1] But digital tools are presenting conceptual changes for publishing too, and some of these are quite unexpected. A small but growing body of evidence suggests that small printed magazines are quietly thriving even as the global newspaper and book industries falter.[2] These publications are being made by young, independent publishers trained to take advantage of the flexibility of digital production tools, but seeking to experiment with print media. They rely on digital networks and business strategies, even when the texts produced become printed matter. Some, like *Sneaker Freaker* (Melbourne, founded in 2002)[3], have achieved longevity and international acclaim

---

[1]   For more on the consequences of these changes for the small publishing sector see Bradley et al. (2011); Hamilton (2011).

[2]   Evidence for this is partly drawn from my own experience over three years studying the field and observing the increase in Australian and international publications over this time. It is challenging to measure the growth of the small publishing sector because small print runs and irregular distribution methods mean they escape the attention of the audit bureaus. I would point to several recent studies of the field which suggest the small press is enjoying a period of growth. In particular see, Freeth (2007); a short but illuminating article from Jacovides (2003); and more recently a survey from MediaFinder.com reporting that 133 magazines launched during the first six months of 2012 with the largest number coming in the local interest and food categories.

[3]   Hereafter all the independent magazines cited will have the city of creation and year of first publication included in brackets after first mention in text.

thanks to a unique focus on what might otherwise be considered ephemeral (in this case providing sport shoe enthusiasts with a definitive catalogue of the market's best and brightest). Others, such as *Offscreen* (Melbourne/ Berlin, 2011), are more recent and more considered about the opportunities the web creates to make print experiences matter. *Offscreen* describes itself as 'a print magazine for pixel people', examining the world of digital business and design in print. The magazine's creator, Kai Brach, was inspired to leave behind his role as a web designer in favour of learning first hand the business of magazine publishing, pushing back against what he describes as the 'ephemerality of digital' (Braich 2012). Despite different approaches, both these magazines are examples of how entirely independently produced Australian publications are being published in print, and satisfy the interests of a readership that might accurately, if awkwardly, be called the global niche. They are only two examples of the growing field of independent magazines using digital know-how to embrace print and find international readerships.[4]

The rise of online and digital publishing by small groups and individuals, looking to take literary success into their own hands, comes as no surprise to anyone familiar with the self-publishing success stories of Amanda Hocking or E.L. James. But one could be forgiven for expecting that the future of publishing in a format such as the small magazine would be bleak. After all, the raison d'etre of such publications is the promotion of new writers, new outlooks and new ideas; in a new media landscape where writers are no longer hostage to the whims of editors and publishers, and where publishing is being radically democratised, can this really be a sustainable proposal for print? Furthermore, given that multinational publishing giants are themselves limping towards dissolution as markets dry up, how could a small magazine with a readership of a few thousand, or even a few hundred, expect to survive?

Yet, as the economic structures that created the contemporary publishing industry are supplanted by new models for delivering content, the barriers that traditionally kept self-publishers and entrepreneurs out of the game are collapsing. Digital communications have been responsible for presenting the creative possibilities of publishing to a wider range of participants. With the explosion of digitally led creativity and amateur/professional co-productions in media making there has been a proliferation of idiosyncratic,

---

[4]   For an excellent survey of the international scope of this trend see Le Masurier (2013).

small-scale creative projects.[5] This is particularly true in the Australian market where the number of small print publications enjoyed a spike over the last decade (Freeth 2007, 19).

This boosted output of local publications has not gone unnoticed by the media. In 2007, Melbourne based newspaper, *The Age*, noted that the enthusiasm for niche small magazines had reached the status of a cultural trend: 'These days, the coolest kids don't play guitars: they start up magazines' (Bailey 2007). In another piece headlined 'Damn the doom, hope is out there', a journalist observed that these new young publishers were:

> ... so enthusiastic about their craft, so willing to learn, so eager to try something new. They help each other out and they bounce back again and again from cold realities. And if the world won't publish their work – hey, they'll start up a magazine and publish it themselves. (Sullivan 2009, 29)

Such enthusiasm is certainly indicative of optimism and creativity on the part of young publishers, but does this publishing activity necessarily translate to print culture being either a fashion-conscious retro signifier for the digital generation or an uncomplicated return to an ideal field of print publishing untroubled by the demands of the modern marketplace? To my mind, such considerations of the flourishing of small publishing enterprises ignore the complex interdependency of online and print media in the creation of content and audiences. Interpreting the present rejuvenation of print culture as a sign of solidarity with traditional publishing risks oversimplifying the cultural economy surrounding these publications. The current crop of small-scale, independent magazines is better considered in empirical terms: these enterprises provide illustration of ways in which newer digital communication tools (from multi-function mobile devices to blogs or social networks) are catalysts for broader experimentation across a range of media. The growth of independent small magazines needs to be understood in the context of the broader phenomenon of the blossoming of small-scale creative projects taking place in creative hub-cities scattered across globe. Although the format of the little magazine goes back to the beginning of print media and the rise of the magazine in the 18th century, accounting for the current proliferation of low-circulation, high-production

---

[5]   The works of Lawrence Lessig and Henry Jenkins provide some of the best-known case studies of the growth in co-creative digital media making. See for example: Lessig (2004, 2001); and Jenkins (1992, 2006).

independent print publications requires us to consider recent cultural, social and political conditions, not only historical antecedents.[6] That is the aim of this article. The reasons behind the growth in printed small magazines are complex, reflecting shifts in the economics of publishing, and, importantly, even greater shifts in the philosophy governing publishers themselves. Where once the skills and infrastructure required to publish books and magazines were concentrated and expensive, technological change has democratised both. Desktop publishers can operate from a suburban bedroom, while the changing economics of printing (and in Australia's case, the nation's proximity to cheap printing services in China) have made smaller print runs economically viable. The emergence of multiple publishing models from e-publishing to print-on-demand has created an environment very different from one dominated by mainstream publishers and publications. In my research interviewing the creators of many of the recent wave of small independent magazines based in Australia, and in reading the archive of interviews and articles with local and international small publishers available online, certain themes come to the fore with regards to the motivation for publishing in print: the ease of access to technologies of production; an entrepreneurial rationale endorsed by the discourse of creative industries; a cultural turn towards individualism and independence that manifests itself in the celebration of smallness as a sign of sincerity; and an aesthetic interest in the material characteristics of print culture. Given these trends, I suggest, the vitality demonstrated by the creators of the current wave of small magazines has at least as much to do with the turn to cultural industries and the development of digital and material literacies as with a romantic infatuation with or social alliance to the traditional field of publishing.

Defining Features

Exactly how many publications make up this group of new, small magazines isn't a simple question. Because some last only a few issues before folding and some appear at irregular and unpredictable intervals, their numbers are difficult to measure. Most would be described as 'amateur' projects in so far as they are labours of love for an individual or a group serving as combined publisher, editor and designer. However, despite this amateur tag, the skills required are usually born of professional training and some experience in

---

6   For a thorough exploration of the historical antecedents of the small press sector see the excellent three-volume work by Brooker and Thacker (2012).

the industry.[7] The focus in content might be short fiction, gastronomy, visual arts, current affairs or popular culture; it may be a collection of writings (fiction, non-fiction, poetry) all linked by a common theme. Despite this diversity, these publications are far from the idiosyncratic zines that were part of the earlier wave of small press publishing in the 1980s and 90s. Although they may be niche publications, they are intended to be commercially viable within the market. Although readerships for these magazines are small, they are internationally spread, and evidence suggests audiences are increasing (LeMasurier 2013). This is especially important for these magazines because the funding support that was once the lifeblood for small publishing enterprises in Australia is notably absent from these newer small magazines (even though this support still underwrites the existence of many of Australia's better known independent publications such as *Overland* and *Meanjin*). Thus – although these publications are sometimes compared with zines on one end of the spectrum, and with established journals at the other – they represent an innovation on earlier independent press models and they are distinct. According to magazine scholar Megan Le Masurier, the new crop of independent magazines are unique because they occupy 'a zone of small-scale creative commercial publishing between DIY zines and mainstream niche consumer magazines' (ibid., 2).

From Politics to Aesthetics

A passing glance at the history of Australia's best-known independent journals reveals that occupying an independent position outside the mainstream of society and culture is central to the identity of such publications; this position underwrites their larger political and aesthetic goals. By way of illustration, consider *Overland*, perhaps the best known of Australia's long-running, independent journals. In its early years in the 1950s *Overland* had close connections with the Communist Party, and although the magazine's association with the party dissolved in 1958, it continues to publish anti-establishment writing and political and social commentary. As the journal says on its website, it is committed to giving:

> … a voice to the experiences that are excluded from the mainstream media and publishing outlets … [as] part of an ongoing attempt to document lesser-known stories and histories, dissect media hysteria

---

7   Regarding this tendency for independent media creatives to consider their occupation a mix of professional/amateur work see Leadbeater and Oakley (1999, 20); Leadbeater and Miller (2004); Beegan and Atkinson (2008); Hamilton (2011).

and dishonesty, debunk the populist hype of politicians, give a voice to those whose stories are otherwise marginalised, misrepresented or ignored, and point public debate in alternative directions. (*Overland*)

Contrast this to the declarations of more recently produced Australian magazines and a picture of the changing politics of independent publishing emerges. While the small magazines created in recent years also take their role as venues for alternative voices seriously, the politics behind their drive towards publishing is less explicitly aligned with discourses surrounding media control and power. Consider, for example, a statement from the publishers of *Collect* magazine (Adelaide, 2010), a small format, full colour magazine of articles and photo essays devoted to 'rejuvenation, interesting places and celebrat[ing] good people': 'We like to think that the future is small, and we want our readers to know the people in their neighbourhood, even if they are only ideological neighbours' (*Collect*). Such sentiments suggest that personal politics is the primary system of value. Here, independent media means exercising self-determination regarding one's personal principles and mode of lifestyle; the idea is as much an aesthetic as a political concept. This attitude is also advanced by Zoe Dattner, the co-publisher of the Melbourne literary anthology *Sleepers Almanac* (Melbourne, 2006) and former president of the Small Press Network (SPN):

> Regardless of their size, small publishers love to provide a location for writing that doesn't or can't find a voice in the mainstream media. Which isn't to say that any of their output is restricted to the independent scene, but it does shed light on one thing: small press publishers are artists of sorts, and what they seek to publish is an expression of their artistic temperament, their values towards ideas. (Dattner)

Significantly, all of the twelve independent, small publishers with whom I have conducted qualitative research rejected the suggestion that their publishing may be understood to have political motives. Many publishers noted they were motivated by a desire to nurture new writers and artists, hoping that they would reach a wider audience, but few associated this commitment with a rejection of the mainstream or an embrace of a political stance. Indeed, an overt alignment with conventional politics was viewed with suspicion: as potentially serving only to turn independent publishing into an exercise in elitism. For example, Ronnie Scott, then the publisher and editor of literary and culture publication *The Lifted Brow* (Brisbane/Melbourne, 2007), explained:

I get impatient when people do make those distinctions [between independent and mainstream]. There is often a reverse-snobbery in indie publishing where people think the mainstream must be evil, but the thing is that readers in the end have pretty discerning taste and are much smarter than people in the arts tend to think they are. It's kinda weird the way people who at once (a) lobby for success and (b) are proud of their underground status treat the idea of readership – at worst, it's really condescending and gross. (Scott)

If personal politics and community building take precedence over explicit political declarations and if the division between mainstream and independent publications is perceived by many new publishers as eroded or, at least, irrelevant, what does 'independence' now signify?

From Independence to 'the Independents'

In 1999, two sociologists, Charles Leadbetter and Kate Oakley, undertook a report for the United Kingdom social research centre, DEMOS investigating how creative individuals were managing their business interests and creative outputs. The pair identified a prominent set of creative workers they dubbed 'the Independents' who favoured roles outside of large organisations and endorsed the idea of doing it (all) yourself: these people 'are producers, designers, retailers and promoters all at the same time'. The pair talked of a 'thriving ecology' of 'micro-businesses' in areas like 'design, music, fashion, computer graphics and games, film and television' (Leadbetter and Oakley 1999, 9, 11). These independents, they said, aimed small in order to retain creative control. They relied on informal networks of friends and associates to organise their work and were defiantly autonomous, uninterested in corporate backing or state subsidies. Although Leadbetter and Oakley didn't explicitly cite publishers in their list, the small publishing projects that make up the subject of this article easily fall into the list of creative activities undertaken by this group. Indeed, the new independent small publishing boom offers an important case study documenting the increasing value and popularity of independent creative work and the way in which the overt political cast to independence is changing, becoming part of a project of personal politics rather than a broad social project.

In their report, Leadbetter and Oakley identify the key ingredients that characterise the work of the Independents. '[T]hey prize their small-scale for the basis for the intimate and creative character of their work. They opt for micro-entrepreneurship because independence will give them a sense of authorship and ownership: it is the best way for them to develop their own work' (ibid., 22). Tellingly, the pair's use of the terms 'authorship' and 'ownership' to describe the nature of this independent work suggest that the self-publishing writer (a figure with a long history of doing-it-yourself) serves as a useful metaphorical model for many modes of contemporary creative entrepreneurship, not only publishing. Although traditional production models continue to offer some advantages (such as well-established distribution, and marketing channels), for an increasing number of creative individuals familiar with the standards and values of the digital economy, these advantages are perceived to be of diminishing worth. The motto of our times says that 'doing it yourself' (or, as John Hartley would have it, 'doing it with others') is now preferable (Hartley 2009, 106).

This attitude was confirmed in my research. Small publishers understood 'independence' to be a strategy for avoiding the unpalatable, frustrating or difficult aspects of mainstream markets, while also suggesting a commitment to positive social and cultural values associated with collective enterprises. For example, Rose Michael, from the small publishing house Arcade Publications (Melbourne, 2007), explained her decision to co-found the press with two other colleagues in terms of the opportunity it afforded them to make creative choices for themselves rather than listening to the wisdom of corporate strategy. That process also allowed them to work closely, communicate clearly and form close ties: 'Having worked in larger companies, you have so many decisions made by committee, and things are owned by so many different areas. In micropublishing, you are able to just kind of do stuff around an island bench' (Murray quoted in Catterson 2009). Liz Seymour the co-publisher of *Stop, Drop and Roll* (Melbourne, 2009, now defunct) made a similar observation about the advantages of being small-scale: 'When no one is paying enough attention to have expectations, you can pretty much carry on doing whatever you do, under cover of anonymity' (Seymour).

Leadbetter and Oakley observe that this desire to go under the radar reflects a more matter-of-fact attitude to the realities of working in a creative field. Not wishing to be caught in the red tape of bigger organisations doesn't mean Independents don't want to create successful, market-ready products. Today '[t]hese independents are negotiating a space within the market economy where they can pursue their interests and develop their own products. Their acceptance of the market is pragmatic. They are not ideologically committed to it: they see it as the best way to pursue what they want to do' (Leadbetter and Oakley 1999, 22–23). Their pragmatism extends to the idea that creative projects should prove themselves self-sustaining in the marketplace. Although their work may not be made *purely* or *primarily* for commercial gain, the new small magazines are made for sale, and their creators hope to find paying audiences.[8] In several interviews different publishers spoke to me regarding their opposition to grants and funding, suggesting that such support gives magazines 'less of an incentive to sell copies to readers, which to my mind involves publishing electrifying writing of one type or another – whether that's writing that's challenging, or writing that's popular' (Scott). Another noted, '… we find grant dependence problematic. We want to try to make the publication as efficient as possible, not wasteful with expenses' (Flynn). Put simply, some publishers felt that grants undermined a publication's ability to be thoroughly independent and responsible to its readership. These publishers felt that their success as independent publishers relied upon the principles of self-sustainability and community relevance: standing on one's own two feet and finding paying support from their readers.

In the case of small publishing some of this reader support came through the publisher's recognition that print was not enough. The success of online forums for establishing likeminded global communities means that small presses need to provide more direct, local community experiences in order to assert the unique character of their creative project. Through public events such as readings and launch parties many small publishers are closely engaged with the lives of their readers. In this respect they exemplify another of Leadbetter and Oakley's observations: the preference for diffusion and collaboration in small independent operations. For example, Arcade Publication's emphasis on the pleasurable intimacy of small publishing also finds expression in community events and public activities which they use to promote their work and the work of others in their local area. In collaboration with other local businesses, they produce walking tours of Melbourne and stage public events and activities to promote and celebrate the vibrant creative cultures to which the city is home: 'We all love a good event, and the purpose of our public activities is mostly about creating community around our publishing output. Storytelling is not a solitary activity' (Dale Campisi[9] quoted in Catterson 2009). For Arcade, publishing is just one aspect of the organisation.

---

[8]   'Anti-commercial … they are not' notes Jacovides (2003, 16).

[9]   Dale Campisi is co-publisher at Arcade Publications.

Although little magazines have always served as spaces for shared sentiment and taste, in recent years this role has taken on a slightly different
cast. According to Leadbetter and Oakley, independent creators express a
preference for creative practice that blurs the lines between production and
consumption: a process of borrowing, mixing, and refining. This technique
of refinement has particular resonance to the publishing industry with its
long tradition of editing. Of course, this more recent model for editing isn't
driven by the standards of neutrality and objectivity that we understand as
essential to the work of copy-editing and fact-checking, but rather borrows
from the creative editorial work of the literary editor (that is, a 'taste maker',
in the model of someone such as Maxwell Perkins, the man who 'made'
Fitzgerald and Hemingway). This is not a new phenomenon: editors and
publishers have always enjoyed their role as cultural tastemakers, however,
terms like 'curation', 'collection' and 'aggregation' have become part of the
everyday lexicon for describing creative engagement via digital media.
Blogs, Tumblr, Twitter, Pinterest and Facebook are all testament to the
daily habits of editing and publishing that are central to contemporary
'digital literacy'. In the case of independent small magazines, for instance,
publishers understand their role as editors of content as central to their
work as participants in a cultural community: they are driven to produce a
publication in order to deliver something that is relevant to their community's interests, and present it in a manner that is meaningful to them and
receive their collaboration and support. It is not insignificant that as we have
observed an increase in these habits among consumers of digital media we
have also seen increases in small press publication:

> Everyone wants to be a writer, but increasingly, everyone wants to be
> an editor, too. Everyone thinks that they have some special vision only
> they can usher into the world ... As an editor, I get it, the desire to
> start a magazine. Editing is awesome, and being able to discover work
> and shape issues the way you want is fun and interesting. I've learned
> so much as an editor and hope I have the privilege of doing it for a
> long time to come. And yet, I also think, another new magazine? ...
> Another magazine where the editors don't know how they're going to
> fund each print issue? Are these magazines, multiplying exponentially,
> really going to offer something we've never seen before? Is becoming an
> editor really that important? (Gay 2011)

Rather than considering the revival of small magazines as evidence of
a print rebellion opposing the exponential growth of digital media, the

desire to edit and curate in print serves as material practice of the editing, synthesising and assemblage that have been encouraged in the era of co-creative digital media culture[10]. Print publishing provides tangible ways to further develop habits stimulated in digital culture. When Sean Wilson, co-publisher of *Stop, Drop and Roll*, explained how he came up with the design and content for the magazine he cited frankly, 'friends and the internet' (Wilson).

From Reading to 'Material Literacy'

While the making, distributing, publicising and proliferation of these publications has been enabled by digital technologies, and their content and aesthetic approach draws on digital cultures, their focus also includes careful attention to what it is about the print format that digital formats can't approximate. While big publishing houses are looking for ways to mobilise their texts across platforms and devices (iPhone, iPad, Kindle, et al.) and mainstream magazines are blending borders between their print editions and lively websites with unique digital content intended to extend the reach of readership, the newer independent publishers have taken an alternative path. They consider the fixity of their printed content an important aspect of their work. *Offscreen*'s Kai Braich summarises the attitude, explaining:

> One of the reasons why I started *Offscreen* was my discontent with the ephemerality of digital. Projects I worked on for many weeks of my life usually disappeared with the next update or clients butchered my work once it fell into the hands of their in-house dev team. Unwrapping a new issue of *Offscreen* still has this magical moment of knowing that this item I created will exist forever in exactly this format. Taking something from idea to screen to the real world is a satisfying experience

---

[10] Examples of the rising popularity and broadening scope of the term 'curation' include a recent book by Steven Rosenbaum, *Curation Nation: How to Win in a World Where Consumers are Creators* (New York: McGraw Hill, 2011) and the swelling enrolments globally in university courses dedicated to studying curatorship; see Pfeiffer, Alice. 2012. 'Who Wants to Be a Curator?' *New York Times* 10 Oct <http://www.nytimes.com/2012/10/11/arts/11iht-rartcurating11.html?_r=0>. Even *Details* magazine noted the trend, quoting the highly celebrated and highly narcissistic musician Kanye West: 'If I had to be defined at this point I'll take the title of an inventor or maybe curator.' <http://www.details.com/culture-trends/critical-eye/201103/curator-power-move-trend#ixzz2d3rBQ6yL>. This new conception of curation is outlined by the artist Jonathan Harris in his TED talk 'The Web as Art,' December 2007, in which he suggests that the compression and disposability of information in the digital age encourages the habits of curation and self-promotion among the users of digital media formats: <http://www.ted.com/talks/jonathan_harris_collects_stories.html>.

no app or website can exceed. This became particularly clear when I saw someone on the train reading my magazine. It's a sense of ownership and craftsmanship that was previously unknown to me. (Braich 2012)

With *Offscreen*, as with all the other publications mentioned above, core elements of the printed text are pushed to the foreground: the quality and tactility of the paper, format, size and binding, the integration of words, images and blank space, along with the publication's function as a material object. These elements often hold conceptual significance to their creators. These material features demonstrate a self-consciousness regarding the publication's position as an old media artefact born of new media cultures. For example, the first issue of the art magazine *Higher Arc* (Melbourne, 2011) featured a play on *Time* magazine's well recognised logo and cover design (in this case the logo was inverted and a large 'unsmiley face' featured on the cover next to a red cross). Inside, the magazine pursued this theme of 'looking back in order to look forward' by surveying a range of now defunct publications from around the world.[11] In a similar spirit, *Ampersand* (Melbourne, 2008) has long favoured a small pocket sized format reminiscent of the original Penguin paperbacks and incorporates aspects of that famous design into each issue.

This embrace of the possibilities of the print medium is not exactly new. Part of a larger transformation of the material culture of the physical book that is being driven by its displacement by the virtual, it is a process that has been most fully realised in the literary journal *McSweeney's* (the creation of the unconventional American author and designer, Dave Eggers) which has been, at various times, a box, a pile of mail and a collection of comics. Fortified by such examples of the possibilities of desktop publishing and the decreasing cost of boutique printing, small magazines in Australia and around the globe are more confidently asserting their value as aesthetic artefacts.

In an environment where publishing, and the media more generally, are undergoing transformation on an unprecedented scale, the magazine format and its value are inevitably altered: since print isn't the only way to reach an audience the medium is less likely to be valued exclusively as a means of communication; that is, it assumes a new role as a stylistic mode. As the designer and theorist Craig Mod suggests,

---

[11]   The phrase 'looking back in order to look forward' comes from the introductory material in the first issue of *Higher Arc*, 2011.

> As the publishing industry wobbles and Kindle sales jump, book romanticists cry themselves to sleep. But really, what are we shedding tears over? We're losing the throwaway paperback. The airport paperback. The beachside paperback. We're losing the dregs of the publishing world: disposable books … These are the first books to go. And I say it again, good riddance … You already know the potential gains: edgier, riskier books in digital form, born from a lower barrier-to-entry to publish. New modes of storytelling. Less environmental impact. A rise in importance of editors. And, yes – paradoxically – a marked increase in the quality of things that do get printed. (Mod 2010)

Print is no longer a delivery technology but an important component of the publication's content or meaning.

There would be no point to this emphasis on the features of print design unless there was a readership to appreciate this focus. New independent magazines rely upon readers who are literate, assuming this necessarily involves various forms of digital and material literacy. In the introduction to their collection *Reading Books: Essays on the Material Text and Reading Culture*, Michele Moylan and Lane Stiles suggest that the idea of literacy needs to be opened up, recognising that reading involves not only textual competence but:

> … material competence, an ability to read the semiotics of the concrete forms that embody, shape, and condition the meanings of texts. Bindings, illustrations, paper, typeface, layout, advertisements, scholarly introductions, promotional blurbs – all function as parts of a semiotic system, parts of the total meaning of a text. (Moylan and Stiles 1996, 2)

Importantly, this consciousness of materiality actually seems to be increasing as readers encounter more and more apparently *dematerialised* texts. In the era of iPhones and Instagram the return to hands-on hobbies among young people (including the production of low-circulation, independent print publications) is proving to be one of the more popular expressions of this interest in old-fashioned habits. A recent article from the fashion and style section of the *New York Times*, charted the revival of the manual typewriter by young, hip writers and designers.

> In more than a dozen interviews, young typewriter aficionados raised a common theme. Though they grew up on computers, they enjoy prying at the seams of digital culture. Like urban beekeepers, hip knitters and

other icons of the D.I.Y. renaissance, they appreciate tangibility, the object-ness of things. They chafe against digital doctrines that identify human 'progress' as a ceaseless march toward greater efficiency, the search for a frictionless machine. (Bruder 2011)

Likewise, an article from the *Age* quoted one local magazine designer and publisher, who accounted for the revived popularity of print by pointing to the banality of technology and the irreplaceable value of materiality:

I use the computer every day to put these together, but I hate computers. There's so many online magazines you can sift through, but there's nothing like the touch and feel of a paper publication, looking through a magazine while you sit at the tram stop or something. (Timba Smitts quoted in Bailey 2007)

In their commitment to the print format, such designers, writers and publishers illustrate the growing interest in material connoisseurship, and particularly a current fascination with the material aspects of literary culture. It is no accident that the content in these publications so often focuses on concepts such as rejuvenation, restoration, collection and preservation. Even outside the sphere of the creative industries, culture at large shows interest in reevaluating the material literacies of literary culture, whether this involves buying Moleskin notebooks or coffee mugs emblazoned with Penguin's famous 'orange stripe' paperback design. The publishers of *Collect*, for example, describe their motivations by saying, 'We make the magazine because we believe in the print medium and know nothing is dead if it's done right' (*Collect*).

However, allegiance to print should not be misinterpreted as a statement against digital communication tools. The renewed impulse to compose using a typewriter or publish in a print format is, rather, facilitated by the expansion of digital technology and cultures. Richard Lanham notes how 'desktop publishing has made typographical layout and font selection matters of everyday expressive concern. We no longer take them as givens; we can make the choices ourselves, and thus we become ever more conscious that they are *choices* and that other choices might be made' (my emphasis) (Atkinson 2006). This attention to textual choices and to the value of the limits that print can impose comes after a period of considerable experimentation (for better and worse) with how the written word can be represented via screens of various types. Several of the small publishers in my research case studies explained how they came to value the print format as a consequence of their experiences producing and consuming in digital media design culture: 'I can't even think in terms outside the internet! I love print, and I think I owe my love of it to everything I've learned from life online', one noted somewhat confessionally.

As David Thorburn and Henry Jenkins remind us, in periods of technological and cultural transition, 'the actual relations between emerging technologies and their ancestor systems proved to be more complex, often more congenial, and always less suddenly disruptive than was dreamt of in the apocalyptic philosophies that heralded their appearance' (Thorburn and Jenkins 2003, 2). Although the emphasis on the distinction of the printed object suggests a rejection of the digital, the preference for print is born of a refusal to see print and online content as opposing camps. Thus, the spread of material literacy is actually a somewhat surprising extension of the ubiquity of digital literacy. In producing printed works that rely upon digital networks for promotion, distribution, discussion, and community building, contemporary small publishers are affirming that the material and the online world are interrelated and interact in mutually beneficial ways.

Conclusion

Publishing has always enjoyed an idiosyncratic relationship with technology: in the early days of what was to become the United States, small printing presses were considered solely for the entertainment of young children. Many of that nation's most important political and polemical documents (such as the writings of Thomas Paine, urging for independence from Britain) started life on those toy presses. Several centuries later, a range of equally unlikely intersections between technology and culture have given birth to very particular independent publishing experiments: in the late 1970s and early 1980s the office photocopier assisted zine makers in cheaply producing multiple copies of their handcrafted publications; by the end of the decade the personal computer and the easy-to-use Word Perfect software encouraged authors to see the potential in self publishing; and by the end of the 1990s the portable networked computer with wifi internet connection gave internet users the freedom to think of themselves as bloggers. By 2010, the ubiquity of the internet as a communications hub, combined with the popularity of Apple products that provide straightforward self-production across video, music, and written media formats has meant that any individual can establish and manage their own creative enterprise. This technological change has come about at a time when creativity and flexibility have acceded to the positions of highest priority for working life. The revival of the print format could be easily dismissed as marginal, fashion conscious and ephemeral or else championed as offering a resistance movement against the inevitability of digital media. But both approaches fail to appreciate how these recent print publications are the products of creators shaped by a cultural doctrine which endorses technology as a ubiquitous, constructive and empowering tool. These publishers advocate for self-employment, entrepreneurialism and a collaborative model of production among their peers not because they seek to return to the golden age of publishing, or because they imagine that an editorial board serves the same role as a garage band – they have chosen these projects because they believe large structures and big business are inflexible, unreliable and unrewarding. The current small press renaissance does not appear to be preoccupied by fidelity to the past; indeed it seems resolutely against the idea of looking backwards, as Johnny Temple, the publisher of Akashic Books and bassist for the indie band Girls Against Boys told a journalist:

> We in the publishing business need to complain less about how no one reads and accept the fact that culture changes. This is a good thing – popular culture evolves. A lot of people seem to long for the good old days back when literature mattered and only straight white men got published … It's a good thing that our culture has moved on from those days in the 50s and 60s and that now there is a much greater diversity of voices that can be published. We need to embrace cultural and technological change. It's our mandate to keep up with the time and stop wishing that culture had stopped evolving 40 years ago. (Temple quoted in Boog 2007)

Chapter 6

A DEMOCRATIC MOMENT – OR MORE OF THE SAME?

New Literary Magazines in Australia, 2005–2012

Phillip Edmonds

The history of literary magazines in Australia has often been the story of committed individuals who started publications to further particular ideological agendas. I will argue here that many have germinated during 'democratic' and optimistic periods, such as in the 1970s, and, more recently, from 2005 to the present day. Such 'democratic' periods were characterised by broad cultural upsurges, the promotion of a range of new writers and a significant increase in the number of publications. There were attempts to create a broader range of magazines other than the 'established' stalwarts such as *Meanjin*, *Overland*, *Southerly*, *Quadrant* and the *Australian Book Review* (*ABR*). Those magazines are 'established' in the sense that they have survived periods of ideological and economic change.

The 'democratic' outbreak of the 1970s, for example, saw the creation and survival for a brief time of *New Poetry*, *Aspect*, *Makar*, *Contempa*, *Tabloid Story*, *Fitzrot*, *Rigmarole of the Hours*, *Luna* and *Dodo*, among many others, a phenomenon that has been commented on in relation to the cultural and political experiments of the decade.[1] Here I wish to largely concentrate on the moment from 2005 to 2012, as the expediential changes of this period are now beginning to be discussed. I will survey the time to enlarge on themes foreshadowed in Stuart Glover's 2011 article, 'No Magazine is an Island: Government and Little Magazines'.

Of interest is that both these 'moments' coincided with revolutionary developments in the informational means of production: in the 70s, the

---

[1] For a detailed survey of the period, *see* Denholm 1979.

advent of cheaper offset printing, and, from the 90s onwards, computerised technology and the internet. Yet even with such technological change, most of the magazines have relied on voluntary labour and an idealism that has often proven unsustainable. Even so, those that have survived have created 'surplus value' in terms of publication credits for individuals and organisations – a topic which needs further discussion in another place.

The outbreak of the early years of the 2000s began with the formation in Brisbane in 2003 of the *Griffith Review*, a new magazine created outside the Sydney–Melbourne nexus, and intensified after 2005 with the formation of a number of new journals, such as *Harvest*, *The Lifted Brow* and *Wet Ink* (created in 2005, around the time Sleepers Publishing was established in Melbourne). A more recent newcomer has been *Kill Your Darlings* in Melbourne. Since 2005, a number of online journals, including *Cordite*, have also entered the field, while others have disappeared.

As I have suggested, the relative cultural hegemony of the established magazines has reigned supreme in that they (due to continued visibility) are seen as *the* magazines. *Meanjin*, *Southerly*, *ABR*, *Overland* and *Quadrant* have, for over 50 years, been granted the great majority of Literature Board assistance and other sponsorship, and been regarded as *the* Australian literary magazines by the weekend papers and on the ABC. It has therefore been in the interests of the Australia Council to support them and provide them with the ability to pay contributors and, due to other forms of subsidy, employ paid staff. *Heat* also joined this group during the 1990s, as did *Island* (formerly *The Tasmanian Review*), but both magazines received lower levels of funding.

For all of the above, assistance has been modest (leaving aside support from arts ministries at a state level, and other forms of subsidy). The average level of Australia Council subsidy is currently approximately $60,000 per annum for the established journals, roughly the equivalent of two postgraduate scholarships. The production of creative writing, in the universities at least, is, then, way out of balance with the resources devoted to its publication and dissemination.

Sleepers established its annual fiction publication, *The Sleepers Almanac*, in 2005, in a climate in which commentators were lamenting a lack of publishing opportunities for new writers, and where CW (creative writing) courses were booming in universities and colleges around Australia, inevitably setting up unrealised demand. *Wet Ink* set itself up partly to cater for that unmet demand, and later in the decade, as I have already noted, in Melbourne (traditionally the home of the little magazine), *Harvest*, *Etchings*, *The Lifted*

Brow and *Kill Your Darlings* were created, in a relatively optimistic economic climate. There have also been other journals of differing configurations with less lofty ambition and visibility.

Despite the advances in digital printing – in terms of short runs and print on demand for 'non-commercial' books – print magazines still have to produce a designated number of copies for subscribers and retail sales, thus making them a relatively cumbersome product without the potential flexibility and timelessness of the book. Even so, the magazines I have mentioned produced good-looking, multicoloured publications during a period when cultural consumers expected high design values. None looked ephemeral or cheap, unlike many of the magazines of the 70s, which, other than the established journals, were often stapled by hand, poorly printed and unable to achieve longevity, and certainly not the reliable commodification required to challenge the established journals.

It could be claimed that by 2005, the main magazines had become blasé and, to an extent, comfortable. Although, non-political in the strictest sense, *Wet Ink* was a utopian gesture, a magazine that wanted to be a CW publication without academic pretensions. It endeavoured to look like a magazine (thus similar in shape to *ABR* and *Overland*) and not like a 'book', and to try not to be too dependent on grants and subsidies – the latter being a factor that would contribute to its eventual demise. *Wet Ink* managed to attract advertising over its first five years, but that was severely curtailed by the first global financial crisis. Although good-looking, its commodification was limited by its penchant for new writers who were not then known to the reading public. It was also primarily a fiction journal during a period when publishing non-fiction was seen as desirable, particularly in the case of the *Griffith Review*, which published themed issues.

The first editorial in *Wet Ink* accused cultural policymakers of lacking insight:

> Thirty years after the innovations of the Australia Council, the limited level of international success some Australian authors have achieved has become a self-satisfied mantra in publishing and arts administration. We believe that the production of CW requires positive outlets of dissemination, rather than being continually marginalised, for better or worse, in universities. (Edmonds and Wilson 2005, 1)

These were brave words, unlike the editorials in *Harvest*, *The Lifted Brow*, *Etchings* and, later, *Kill Your Darlings*, which were largely author-centred. *The Lifted Brow* is still with us and pretty interesting (after an interregnum during 2011), while *Harvest* appears to be an occasional publication, as does *Etchings*. *Heat* ceased publishing in early 2011, and *Wet Ink* in September 2012.

This 'democratic' moment, then, was facilitated by healthy economic conditions; but the global financial crisis of 2008–9, and, currently, its lingering effects, have presented challenges. For instance, the opportunity and onslaught of online, and its deconstruction of the marketability of the printed word, has coincided with a weakening economy. Other tendencies have also been at work: the continuance of 'the celebrity moment' across popular and 'private' culture; a desire for a representational shorthand to explain the nature of the current crisis in late capitalism (that is, a desire to wish away the crisis of economic 'value' under layers of spin); and counterintuitive bureaucratic moves in higher education, which are of relevance because Australian universities have always been engaged, in one way or another, with literary magazines.

So, by the close of the first decade of the 2000s, a confluence of contradictory opportunities and factors were impacting on the magazines. During 2010 and 2011, the Australian Research Council (ARC) engaged in a process of ranking journals – A, B, C and lower – on a scale of perceived prestige. Some journals wished to participate, others did not, and new journals without a track record were disadvantaged. In any case, an 'anti-democratic' moment arose, one that would possibly work against future motivation, harm 'non-academic' journals and discourage writer-academics from writing for new journals. As a case in point, under the current ARC guidelines, no Excellence in Research for Australia (ERA) points are allocated to academics to edit either refereed or non-refereed journals. Peter Shergold (2011) put it this way: '[I]t's scarcely surprising that a direct contribution to public policy is generally not viewed highly by most academics or universities in which they work.' This is concerning, because there is a large group of CW academics who wish to publish their creative work as research.

It was noted by other commentators that the ranking system bore little resemblance to its 'real-world' implications, and that scholars were being encouraged to 'think small'. Raimond Gaita went further, writing that the 'universities have retreated from the public institutions of culture' (Gaita 2012). These 'anti-democratic' moves (my phrase) are also useful during an era of budgetary restraint – and the internet – so as to encourage disinvestment. In such an environment, the mantra behind online has often been evangelical, when, as I am arguing, close enquiry needs to take account of economic influences.

Some of the analysis regarding the encroaching online environment has offered a 'the medium is the message' line straight out of Marshall McLuhan, against a backdrop where the internet has accelerated capitalism's search for cheap markets and 'creative destruction'.[2] Its innovations, then, are super-efficient for service delivery, but too overarchingly effective to protect the value of labour. An interesting aside is that the New York Stock Exchange is suspicious of Facebook's ability to generate income and its inflated stock price.

Caroline Hamilton articulates this point in different words.

> [C]reative enterprises facilitated by the internet are no more independent from capitalist processes than their traditional counter-parts are ... Workloads but not budgets have increased, just as traditional revenue streams (especially advertising) dried up ... (and) content is routinely produced free of charge by the audiences that also consume it. (Hamilton 2011)

Coupled with such advice as she has received from publishers – claims that 'readers and writers can be found anywhere in the world ... so much that sales aren't even a pressure' (ibid.) – the implication is that income is not an issue for writers. Thus, the 'democratic' net moment came at a cost.

Mark Davis noted in 2006 the passing of a generation of 'true believers' in a 'national' literature who one could construe supported the local literary culture and the magazines of the past. Currently, where do the new readers or migratory print surfers come from? Are they mainly other writers and would-be writers in this democratic and undemocratic moment? Is blogging and social media a privatising experience hidden under the rhetoric that gatekeepers have been marginalised? Has a community of writers and readers been so dispersed that the literary magazines will no longer be mobilisation points, even if using the new configurations? Is that even a problem? The popularity of writers' festivals may also represent an aspect of the current, fractious 'democratic' moment, in that, while most of them have become important marketing tools for publishers, they marginalise new writers who aren't invited and become hierarchical reference points for readers. Are they, then, superseding the traditional role of the magazines?[3] Much of what I have described is, of course, taking place against a background where the future for print magazines is generally dire, with

---

2   A term used in Schumpeter 1975.
3   For a discussion of the growing influence of writers' festivals, see Galligan 1999.

sales dropping sharply for even food, celebrity gossip and motor magazines. So will the printed 'literary' magazine as a niche product survive?

For all that, in 2008, Wenche Omundsen and Michael Jacklin identified in their report to the Australia Council on the literary infrastructure of Australia that the magazines were maintaining and developing what they had always done well: providing a springboard for new writers, supporting marginalised literary forms, and so forth (Omundsen and Jacklin 2008). But, the report continued, 'the usual problems remained … limited staff levels, problems gaining more subscribers, and regionalism which plays a role in limiting the reach of certain magazines' (ibid.). Furthermore, will digital technologies overcome these problems in a spectator society? Facebook 'likes' (for example) don't automatically translate into buyers and subscribers.

Hopefully, they will. But it must be noted that journals such as *Cordite* and *Mascara* survive with the ability to pay writers due to Australia Council assistance. They have subscription facilities, but they are free – something that is common mainly among poetry publications. It is extremely difficult to erect paywalls when most magazines provide a great deal of free content on their websites; it is far easier, in fact, to sell ebooks. As Stuart Glover (2011) has suggested:

> So far, the internet hasn't created a viable literary magazine model. Literary magazines have multiplied on the internet, but mostly … they are edited by the unpaid with varying levels of skill. Expertise is costly and is crowded out.

In December 2011, Benjamin Laird surveyed the changes during the latter part of the decade and found that where once social media was seen as an adjunct promotional tool for the printed article, it is now a situation where 'running a quarterly lit journal in 2011 means doing everything you did twenty years ago, plus tweeting, using Facebook, creating blog content, and so forth' (Laird 2011). He was optimistic, but wondered where social media would be in four years, adding that 'in the short history of social sites … popularity can dissipate as quickly as it grows' (ibid.).

Volunteerism, as a notion, then, could be problematic for cooperative gestures in the current climate of individualised promotion, and the literary magazine, as a grouping of interests, and involving a notion of working with and for others, could be under strain as a working idea.

The established journals adapted, and now offer social media and free downloads on their sites. The *ABR*, under pressure from the Australia

Council to convert to digital, has been active, but its content is largely safe and its reviewing policies unadventurous. In spite of the online push, the most visible journals have persisted with the 'monumentalist' look of the book in their hard-copy offerings. In *Meanjin*'s case, the hard-copy option is seemingly a significant retro other to its online presence (at a time when it has recently made some moves towards publishing 'new' writers), while the *Griffith Review* employs a stable of largely well-known commentators and academics. Paradoxically, then, the 'democratic' moment between 2005 and 2012 saw the concentration of even more subsidised resources in the hands of the established magazines, providing them with the time and staff to further promote themselves.

Of the others, *Kill Your Darlings* has made a hipster mix of the mediums, and *Island* persists. *Overland* adapted to both forms, but its print version had for many years run counter to the monumentalism of the other journals, and its content, given its leftist constituency, was riskier and issue-based, reflecting, perhaps, an engagement with what it considers new class formations.

Online, then, reduces the costs of traditional publishing. But different kinds of work have been encouraged, and significantly more time online for editors and other staff makes the issue of viability questionable. It is no longer possible for those involved to work in discrete blocks of time. For *Wet Ink*, even though retail sales were bad (particularly after the closure of Borders) and it could no longer obtain advertising (unlike when it began), the two people who worked most on the magazine could no longer afford to donate their largely voluntary time. The decision to close was financial, as going online would not reduce the workload and wasn't considered a viable alternative.[4]

In a recent blog, Stuart Glover further notes that 'despite decades of funding the reader base for little magazines hasn't grown much, even as the number of titles proliferates' (Glover 2012). He goes on to mention the crop post-2005, raising the issue that Australia Council funds are limited in the current economic climate, all the while suggesting that Australia can't, or won't, support more than a handful of magazines (ibid.). Glover says that the established journals to which I have referred subsist with 500–2000 subscribers, and are propped up by government and institutional support; that the newer magazines will therefore have difficulty paying

---

[4] For a discussion see Edmonds, Phillip. 2013. '*Wet Ink* Past and Future.' *The Victorian Writer* May: 23–25.

authors and attracting writers of quality; and that 'smaller journals … will, I expect, never have enough readers to offer … editors full-time paying jobs' (ibid.). He is aware that the magazines 'could be marked for death or for Promethean transformation', and that, as we have begun to see, 'the internet has meant that magazines are not really issue-bound and time-bound little magazines anymore; instead they are high end-end literary and commentary sites' (ibid.).

But questions about the maintenance of quality material and whether all readers will prefer to dispense with the anticipation factor behind periodic publication will, I suspect, remain. Irrespective of the publishing format, who will be the editors? What will be published, by how many new authors? The newly created online *Review of Australian Fiction* is a case in point, in that it basically commissions work from well-known authors. This is administratively manageable, but is it 'democratic'?

Online magazines will be created, and maybe a few print versions, but the urgencies of the economy will remain, either through the level of grants received or the motivation of people to display loyalty to a publication over a period of time. Furthermore, the institutionalisation of CW in the academy has not, it appears, created more readers or contributed to the health of the magazines.

The current economic crisis – essentially a deferral of toxic credit across the globe masking declining rates of profit in key sectors – is still to conclude, and with it, state and federal arts budgets will be under pressure, reducing governments' ability to support magazines, and in particular any new magazines, if they wish to survive for longer than a few years. In such a climate, discretionary spending will also be under pressure.

For the time being, one can say that the period between 2005 and 2012 was a 'democratic' outbreak, in that opportunities were given to a range of new writers and a few new magazines are still publishing, including the university-subsidised *Griffith Review*. But other initiatives have been mediated and curtailed by a skittish economy and the contradictions of technological change and university politics. Broadly, the period has seen a consolidation of 'more of the same' and the survival of the established journals – those, that is, with the resources to negotiate the multiple subsidies needed for survival.

Chapter 7

A FRAGILE CRAFT

Publishing Poetry in the Twenty-First Century

Kevin Brophy

This paper begins with a broad backward look at views on funding for literature and the arts in Australia. This will form the background to an account of decisions surrounding the Literature Board's funding of poetry publishing in 2010. At the time these threatened to capsize the always-fragile craft that is the publishing house, Five Islands Press. I will not be able to offer the wisdom or insights that might finally resolve problems of viability, or continued vigour and contemporary relevance for poetry publishing, but I hope that this paper will add to a developing picture of how life is for small, independent presses and perhaps how poetry might continue to be an essential aspect of the distinctiveness of the cultural life of Australia.

Arts funding must always justify itself against the many other demands made upon governments' expenditure. This task is always a fraught one, for while the broad value of the arts might be unquestioned, their actual value in money terms is almost impossible to calculate uncontroversially, and without the biasing weight that already-privileged minorities can bring to such a decision-making process. In his 1985 study, *Arguing the Arts*, Tim Rowse traced the history of Australian government arts policy as it shifted in the 1970s towards an acknowledgement that access and participation needed to be balanced against so-called excellence, in distributing arts dollars. This major adjustment did not, though, resolve problems related to increasing audiences and commercial distribution for art forms, nor did it correct in any significant way the imbalances that still exist between the protected arts of, for instance, ballet and symphony companies against the apparently less deserving, cheaper or even dispensable art forms (among which we might include poetry). The debate provoked by Rowse's book and other essays written at this time also brought the possibility of arts funding to support community diversity and geographic regionalism to the fore (see for instance Frow 1986). This field is characterised by a melange of demands that cannot all be satisfied as the scarce resources of government funding are painstakingly distributed. These debates continue into the present with, for example, Caroline Hamilton quoting feisty small press publishers in her 2011 *Overland* article, 'Sympathy For the Devil?' These small publishers are keen to establish niche markets based upon moral responsibility towards an audience and shared enthusiasms with that audience. They are suspicious of the negative effects of state subsidies on what they hope will be commercially viable independent art projects. The internet of the 2000s holds out a promise of flexibility, cheap production and independence, just as the Gestetner did in the 1970s. This suspicion and resistance towards arts funding, and the constant adjustments to the manner of funding in response to the rise of new values in politics and public debate has been typical of the history of arts funding in Australia.

Arts funding has for many years received bad press from journalists and commentators who are determined to ferret out those projects that lend themselves to being presented as indefensible follies. More venomously, arts funding is sometimes painted as a form of undeserved or even corrupt government handouts. Writing in *Quadrant* in 2008, Michael Connor described the Labor Government's increase of support for Indigenous arts as pork-barrelling, and wondered 'what our cultural life would look like without the $156 million the Australia Council distributes … It might even be lively and interesting' (Connor 2008, 7).

These sorts of attacks are made more possible by confusion over those values mentioned above and the specific policies that underpin arts funding in Australia. Arts funding, as indicated, seems to stagger without rigorous policy from minister to minister, while artists and arts bodies hope that occasionally one of these ministers will deeply value the arts. In 2005, when Paul Keating was prime minister he was shocked to learn that his son's music teacher, the internationally renowned Liszt pianist, Geoffrey Tozer, earned $9000 a year and rode a bicycle to work, while Keating's secretary at the time earned nearly four times that much. Keating was moved enough to establish the Australian Artists Creative Fellowships, though at first he excluded writers because literature was not 'art'. It took a phone call from Donald Horne, then Chair of the Australia Council, to convince him to revise his understanding of art (Puplick 2008, 6). This ad hoc initiative followed a pattern, for the original Commonwealth Literary Fund was established in 1906 in response to publicity surrounding the death of the

Celtic-Australian poet and satirist Victor Daley, whose widow was left in poverty after his death (ibid., 7). In 1977 the Fraser Government made the decision that funding of ballet, opera and major theatre in Australia would be reserved for direct Cabinet decisions, on the basis that these art forms were too important to Australia's reputation to be left to arts funding bodies (ibid., 17). This decision was later reversed by the Hawke Government. Nevertheless, at the national level, cultural funding still follows the values of the Fraser Government, with most of it going to symphony orchestras, major theatre companies, opera and ballet (Westbury 2009, 37). Towards the end of his period in office in 2007, John Howard intervened to provide $1.5 million to bail out the Sydney Dance Company, not for the first time. Chris Puplick, who has had a long involvement with the arts as a senator and as a public figure, observed in his 2008 essay on arts funding, 'Decisions about the arts tend to be made in isolation and without regard for any masterplan' (Puplick 2008, 4). Compounding this problem is the conservatism of this shifting mosaic of funding models, which means for instance that graphic novelists and video artists fall between those known art forms that bureaucracies understand and fund (Westbury 2009, 39).

This endemic lack of a vision for the arts in Australia is not just a problem emanating from politicians, for it is equally a result of artists misunderstanding the political processes in a democracy. Chris Puplick has noted that the arts do not have a national body to represent their interests, such as a peak body that might do for arts what the Australian Council of Social Services (ACOSS), the Confederation of Australian Sport (CAS) or the Council for Humanities, Arts and Social Sciences (CHASS) can do for their constituents. In the arts, advocacy comes surprisingly often from individuals or from splintered specialist groups competing among themselves for the limited funds available, and often unable to appreciate the political reality of voters wanting to know 'why money that is being spent on opera, lesbian drum festivals, or acquiring another Jackson Pollock, is not being spent on their children's school or their neighbourhood hospital' (Puplick 2008, 31). In addition, if the arts sector is to find its way to effective lobbying and effective representation of its arguments at the highest levels, arts advocates need to communicate across the spectrum of the political parties without appearing to be partisan. Without such a level of sophistication, there will always be a roller-coaster dependence upon changes of government and changes of heart among powerful figures.

Recently the work of Richard Florida and others has brought the economic importance of creativity and thus of the arts to public notice in new ways. It has become easier to find a way to argue for a place for the arts in a national profile and a national economy. The city of New York, recognising the economic importance of reputation, cultural intensity, creativity, ideas and their expression, funds its arts sector with a budget almost equal to the Australia Council's (Lacayo 2008, 42).

This brings us to the small Australian poetry publishing house, Five Islands Press. Ron Pretty was the driving force for this press as it established itself in the decades up to 2007 as a fiercely independent and almost frenetically active press. Ron Pretty published over 230 titles in a little over twenty years, including an impressive series of *New Poets* chapbooks linked to national tours and the famous poetry retreats at Wollongong University's coastal campus. When Ron retired in 2007, a small group of poets took up the press, reconstituted it as a non-profit incorporated association, and with some changes of membership it has continued to publish a redesigned series under the now famous imprint. In five years this new group has published 17 titles, our poets winning four major awards (Anne Elder Award, Victorian Premiers Award for Poetry, Wesley Michel Wright Award, and *The Age* Poetry Book of the Year), and being short-listed or highly commended for national and state awards nine times. These awards and short-listings are more than twice the national average for poetry titles subsidised by the Australia Council (McLean and Poland 2010, 31).

With an editing and publishing team of five volunteers the most titles we can manage to publish in a year is three, or at a pinch, four. With no capital behind us, we can only publish if we have Literature Board support. We operate as professionally as possible, with an excellent website, online sales, a Facebook and Twitter presence, a national distributor we check on monthly, book launches in poets' home states and at festivals, a paid designer for text and cover designs, and developing e-book offerings.

In 2010, after three years of successful publishing as this new group under the established banner of Five Islands, we proposed three books to the Literature Board for publication subsidy. These were *This Floating World* by Libby Hart, *Vishvarupa* by Michelle Cahill, and *The Brokenness Sonnets I-III and Other Poems* by Mal McKimmie. We had selected these three manuscripts from nearly a hundred submitted from all over Australia. Our method of selection was that all of us read every manuscript, each of us came up with a long short list, then we re-read and discussed and negotiated until we had consensus.

Libby Hart was a past winner of the Anne Elder Award, and had also been short-listed for the Mary Gilmore Award. She had received Australia

Council support, and had been awarded the Dinny O'Hearn Fellowship at the Australian Centre. *This Floating World* had already won an award as a stage performance. We were excited at the prospect of publishing Libby Hart's book. Mal McKimmie's book was brave and funny and intense. It would be his second collection by Five Islands Press, and it built upon that first book in ways that showed a maturing and confident voice. Michelle Cahill's *Vishvarupa* would be her third book in six years. She was a multiple prize-winning poet with grants and assistance from the Australia Council, Copyright Agency Limited, and Hawthornden Castle Retreat.

The only title the Literature Board supported was Michelle Cahill's book. Other publishers similarly had their publishing projects only part funded or not funded at all in that year. The profile of successful funding applications seemed chaotic, it made no sense to us, on the basis of what had been happening over the past three years. I phoned the Board officers and then sent them an email in July 2010, pointing out that for a press as small as we were, this reduction in activity put our survival at risk, reducing our public presence, making the possibility of attracting further interns or volunteers unlikely because there would be little work to do, and threatening to run down our budget to a point where we could no longer operate viably. Grateful though we were for the support for Michelle's manuscript, we were puzzled that Mal's and Libby's books were not judged worthy of publication, especially considering our rigorous selection process.

We received a reply the next day that informed us there had been a reduction in funding and an increase in the number of titles applied for by publishers. As always, applications were considered against two criteria: the literary merit of the individual title and evidence of the publisher's ability to carry out the proposal to a high standard.

We were informed that in the climate of reduced funding, the Literature Board had put the matter of publishers aside and 'increased' their focus on individual titles. The matter of literary merit 'was heavily scrutinized' (emails 13 July and 19 July 2010). I took this to mean that the assessment panel considered Mal McKimmie and Libby Hart to be among those least worthy of support on the grounds of a relative lack of literary merit. Of course this rankled with us, given the care we had taken in selection, and especially given the outstanding public record of Libby's achievements.

In this email exchange we were also informed that the Literature Board had received in May 2010 a report from a comprehensive review of literature funding in Australia conducted by the University of Western Sydney. This review would be shortly released and requests for feedback issued.

We continued to correspond with the Board officers, reiterating that we wished to do all we could to demonstrate to them that we publish to a high standard, and that we select with considerable care and rigour. On 20 July we received another email from the Board informing us that the Board had set aside funding for 'initiatives to benefit the publishing sector during the 2010/11 financial year'. On 20 September, we received news that the Board had set aside funds specifically for mid-career writers (those who had published at least one and not more than four books), and that these funds were now available for applications *only from publishers who had submitted in the immediate past round.* There would be no public call for applicants for these funds. This new round seemed to be expressly designed to favour the two writers we had unsuccessfully proposed in the previous round. We applied, we were successful, and we have been able to publish the two poetry collections. Mal McKimmie's book won the *Age* Poetry Book of the Year for 2012 and Libby Hart's book was short-listed for both the Victorian Premiers Award and the *Age* Poetry Book of the Year in 2011. On the question of literary merit we felt vindicated. Where those extra funds had come from, why they were seemingly so carefully targeted to us as publishers and to the very writers previously rejected remains something of a mystery.

In October 2010 the Board released *A Case for Literature: The Effectiveness of Subsidies to Australian Publishers 1995–2005*, the report prepared by Dr Kath McLean and Dr Louise Poland from the University of Western Sydney. This report concluded that subsidies were essential to the continued existence of poetry publishing among independent Australian-owned presses operating without capital. The report recommended unsurprisingly that publishing subsidies be increased. In a move that would bring back a system abandoned in the early 1990s, the report recommended that block grants be provided for extended periods in recognition of publishers' overall literary programs. This would allow small presses to develop a vision, and plan for more innovative forms of publishing than the strictly annual promise of printing 250 copies of a single approved title at a time. Flexibility and imagination would become possible.

This then is the present situation. The Literature Board now supports publishers through 'Publishing Program Grants' that can amount to $15,000, $35,000 or for 'special' projects, $50,000 per year. We felt we came through a difficult moment in 2010 with luck and with the benefit of the hard work we had put into our selection of manuscripts, our publishing standards, and our care with applications to the Board. We know, though, that our hard work will never ensure survival, for the craft remains fragile and the gods of the sea capricious, unpredictable, and ultimately political.

The Federal Government recently announced in its 2013/14 budget a significant increase in funding for the Australia Council, meeting at the end of its term a national cultural policy promise to boost funding to the arts. The increase in Australia Council funding is in the order of 15 per cent (though arts and cultural funding in total received an increase of 5.5 per cent). From a previous budget of $188 million the Australia Council is due to receive $219 million in 2013/14, with a total budgeted increase of $75 million over the next four years. It does, however, seem from the detail in the budget that over $18 million of the increase will go towards major companies and the new small-business model ArtStart program. This upward swing will no doubt provide momentum for a downward swing in the not too distant future as arts funding follows its predictably erratic fortunes.

Perhaps the only reasonable protection we could have would be a truly national body, as Chris Puplick has suggested, one that broadly and deeply represents all the arts to the federal government, a body that avoids pitting art form against art form. Its brief would be to develop policy standards that match an inspiring vision for a creative nation. This would be an advocacy body that would work to ensure there are no poor cousins among the arts.

Chapter 8

SMALL PRESS SOCIAL ENTREPRENEURSHIP

The Values of Definition

Aaron Mannion and Amy Espeseth

Most small presses are not motivated either solely or principally by profit, and yet they operate in the marketplace in similar ways to profit driven enterprises.[1] This contradiction has both theoretical and practical consequences. The pseudo-commercial nature of the small press obscures its progressive mission to contribute to our shared cultural life. But small presses' rejection of traditional commercial models also affects their ability to operate effectively and efficiently. This essay applies the model of social entrepreneurship (SE) to small press publishing, as a means of reconciling their idealistic commitment to publishing literary or culturally significant work with the necessarily commercial nature of book production. The insights gleaned chime with both our own experience at Vignette Press and that of the small press peers we have informally surveyed. Our experience is that there is no robust, commonly shared model for the work we do.

---

[1]   It is widely accepted that small presses focused on literary and culturally significant works are not motivated by profit. There is, however, often a misconception that this is a recent phenomenon. As Bill Henderson makes clear in 'The Small Book Press: A Cultural Essential', it has been this way for some time. Henderson's article overviews the history of independent publishing, arguing for its centrality to literary culture. He highlights the role of small presses in the production of notable books including Walt Whitman's *Leaves of Grass*, Upton Sinclair's *The Jungle*, Anaïs Nin's *Winter of Artifice* and the early work of beat poets such as Allen Ginsberg and Lawrence Ferlinghetti. Henderson reveals that these works would probably have vanished without the intervention of the small presses involved; he is also quite clear that profit is not the motivation for the work done by these presses: 'A small press is an alternative to the commercial establishment. Often the press can be a profit making alternative (especially if it concentrates now and then on practical and specialised publications), but usually, for the literary publisher, profit is of minimal interest' (Henderson 1984, 62).

Small publishers often define their operations in the negative: they are not structured like traditional publishers; they are not market driven. It is hoped that this paper helps establish a shared vocabulary that will allow us to clearly articulate what we do. Caroline Hamilton's 'Sympathy for the Devil' has already noted that small publishers operate between the poles of 'commerce and community' (Hamilton 2011, 93). We wish to develop Hamilton's insight further by combining it with existing models of non-profit focused activity within, or parallel to, the commercial sphere.

Before continuing, it's worth emphasising that our focus is on small press publishers engaged in the production of literary or culturally significant works. While even larger Australian independent publishers (such as Scribe Publications and Text Publishing Company) appear committed to Australian literature despite it being a money-losing or break-even proposition, these firms generally operate in an overtly commercial way. We are also not attempting to include publishers funded by larger parent organisations, such as university presses or the publishing arms of non-governmental organisations. We are instead interested in small presses who lose money or whose meagre profit is derived from the substantial unpaid labour of their publishers, editors, designers and contributors. Put simply, our focus is on publishers who are not providing their owners, publishers, editors or contributors with a livelihood. While we are aware that this definition is restrictive, we believe this restriction allows us to retain clarity while still capturing much of this marvellously diverse and idiosyncratic sector.

Presenting a robust model for such organisations presents several material benefits. For one, it provides a shared way of articulating the work of small publishers to funding bodies such as the Australia Council. A model can also provide insights into the effective structuring of such enterprises, illuminating how best to allocate the scant resources available to small presses by making clearer questions such as whether, or how much, to pay authors, and when the costs incurred will negatively affect the marketing

---

Henderson's analysis was conducted in the 1980s, though the works he cites date back to the 19th Century. Nevertheless, Megan Le Masurier notes a similar contemporary disregard for money in her investigation of what she terms 'independent magazines'. She defines independent magazines to include the publications of publishers such as McSweeney's, but also magazines such as *Adbusters* and Melbourne's own, now vanished, *Don't They Shoot Homos?* Le Masurier comments on the failure of such enterprises to largely eschew profit as primary motivation: 'They are made for sale, they may occasionally make money, and a few eventually develop into commercially successful enterprises, but profit seems not to be the initial or primary aim' (Le Masurier 2012, 384.).

and pricing that determine the readership a publication receives.[2] The SE model allows us to see that this question requires a balancing of operational concerns (funding, attracting authors) with an analysis of how the decision will impact on the key stakeholders (writers, readers).

Although SE is a theory not without substantial problems, it offers a robust, recognisable model with the capacity to make clear how small scale individual initiatives contribute to, and interact with, a community committed to common values and goals.[3] SE makes clearer the relationship of a given small press to the interested observers (writers, editors, readers) who are not simply consumers, but who may have no direct hand in production. Indeed, those interested in the flourishing of literary culture often feel they have a stake in the success of presses whose books they rarely read. This may happen when a particular press, or simply the existence of an ecosystem of presses, is thought to buttress our shared culture. Finally, SE makes clear the necessity of community within small press activity, while providing a theoretical framework for the support of those communities.

Social Enterprise, Social Entrepreneurship

As a practice, social entrepreneurship has probably existed since the earliest exchange economies, but the term 'social entrepreneurship' emerged in the 1970s and early 1980s, and is particularly associated with the work of the Ashoka organisation (Mair and Martí 2006). It is used in conjunction, and often interchangeably with, the term social enterprise: for many theorists a social enterprise is simply an example of social entrepreneurship (Chell 2007; Peredo and McLean 2006, 57). Nonetheless, though the terms are often used as cognate, there are those who note significant divergences in usage and theorisation: social entrepreneurship is more often grounded in

---

2   The issue of paying writers has been discussed extensively recently, though rarely with much discrimination. Some representative recent discussions include O'Brien (2013), Larsen (2013), Mills and Laird (2013) and Gilmore (2012).

3   Though we believe SE provides a robust model, it is clear that are many alternative ways to study such enterprises. A straightforward analysis of the financial affairs of individual presses, perhaps coupled with a breakdown of the hours contributed by various participants, would be invaluable. We would, personally, be keen to read an investigation grounded in the work of theorists such Bourdieu, detailing how small presses function as sites for the production of cultural capital. We would be interested to read an examination of whether (and how) cultural capital produced through the work of small press publishing relates directly or indirectly to how those involved earn their livelihoods.

economics and Anglo-American analytic traditions of philosophy, while social enterprise discussions tend to rely more heavily on critical theory and Marxist related thought. Social entrepreneurship literature often emerges from advocates within management and business schools. 'Social entrepreneurship' is often the preferred term of individual and small group enterprises, while 'social enterprise' is favoured by larger scale co-operatives, charities and collectives. Despite the neoliberal connotations of the term,[4] we have decided to focus on social entrepreneurship theory as it better reflects the individual or small group organisation of small press activity. Small press operators may like to think of writers and readers as stakeholders in our enterprise, but they are rarely as engaged in our project as co-operative members or staff in a worker-run business, which constitute the more usual contexts for social enterprise terminology.

Given social entrepreneurship's diverse theorisation, we have chosen to employ Peredo and McLean's synthetic definition of SE, derived from a broad spectrum of theories,[5] which we believe is restrictive enough to provide critical clarity on the concept of SE, but inclusive enough to register the diversity of the small press sector. Their formulation is based on five criteria that mark the social entrepreneurship venture:

> ... social entrepreneurship is exercised where some person or persons (1) aim either exclusively or in some prominent way to create social value of some kind, and pursue that goal through some combination of (2) recognizing and exploiting opportunities to create this value, (3) employing innovation, (4) tolerating risk and (5) declining to accept limitations in available resources. (Peredo and McLean, 56)

---

4   Our understanding of neoliberalism aligns with the definition of David Harvey: 'Neoliberalism is in the first instance a theory of political economic practices that proposes that human wellbeing can best be advanced by liberating individual entrepreneurial freedoms and skills within an institutional framework characterised by strong private property rights, free markets and free trade. The role of the state is to create and preserve an institutional framework appropriate to such practices. [...] State interventions in markets (once created) must be kept to a bare minimum because, according to the theory, the state cannot possibly possess enough information to second guess market signals (prices) and because powerful interest groups will inevitably distort and bias state interventions (particularly in democracies) for their own benefit' (Harvey 2005, 2).

5   Future analyses may well benefit from applying more restrictive definitions. More precise definition would allow more accurate application of the insights and lessons documented in the literature to small press operations. At this stage, however, we were more interested in capturing a broad range of small press operations than culling organisations that did not fit a strict paradigm.

We believe that small presses meet this first criterion, presuming that cultural value is accepted as a form of social value – a position that continued government support of cultural projects presupposes.[6] That being said, the desire to maximise the social value created may be at odds with maximising the cultural value – this is the dilemma in deciding whether to fund grassroots participation in art at the expense of elite practitioners, or support popular art forms rather than 'high' culture. The difficulty in determining this question is compounded, because within SE 'social value' derives its meaning from a number of overlapping frameworks in ways that are rarely well defined. Most important in this respect is the field of social justice (Miller 1999, 8, 186). Social justice is usually believed to be grounded in human rights and is usually concerned with care for disadvantaged groups. But the term social value is also used to designate goods or services that are of value to our common public sphere, such as the development of new ideas and art forms.[7] This kind of social value may make no immediate contribution to less fortunate members of that society. Small presses can more strongly claim to contribute to this second understanding of social value than to the earlier, social justice grounded interpretation.

Small presses may fulfil the second criteria – 'recognizing and exploiting opportunities to create this value' – though how successfully they achieve this varies among organisations. The criteria is itself problematic, because it blurs from a description into an evaluation of success – a recognised fault of many definitions of social entrepreneurship, which are often defined via successful examples (Tan et al. 2003, 8–9; Peredo and McLean). Small presses actively exploit opportunities presented by literary festivals, the shifting priorities of funding bodies and emerging topics of interest. In terms of seizing opportunities, small presses concentrating on the publication of literary or culturally significant work could do better in targeting and cultivating niche markets. Such failures should, however, be put in context. Cultural products possess a depth of identity that means that surface similarities hide significant internal complexity: my collection of working-class short fiction

---

[6]   Arguments against treating cultural goods as social goods are varied. From the right, it is argued that cultural goods are often simply left wing propaganda in artistic clothing. Elements of the left argue that government support for culture is simply middle class welfare. Thinkers such as Peter Singer point out that, from a utilitarian perspective, funding cultural goods is inefficient in reducing suffering and promoting happiness (Singer 2010; Bunting 2010).

[7]   Under this framework, 'social value' is a form of 'social return' defined as 'the sum of the private and external marginal benefits of a unit of human capital' (Lange and Topel 2006, 461).

may be very different to your collection of working-class fiction. It could be argued that niches are targeted and exploited, but that such niches are defined by less obvious criteria such as style rather than more obvious criteria such as subject matter.

The third criterion, employing innovation, also suffers from substituting evaluation for description. What should be taxonomic becomes a judgement of success. Nonetheless, small press publishers do, on the whole, display this characteristic – though innovation is often more apparent in the product (the published work) than in the business model. Innovation exists with business models in cases such as *The Lifted Brow* (who bundle their publication with entry to their launches, launches that include performances by exciting new bands), *Ampersand Magazine* (funded through a Pozible campaign) and the *Australian Review of Fiction* (digital only, short format and low unit cost). Changes in the marketplace, including digital publication, print on demand and the pressure on bricks and mortar bookshops, necessitate the embrace of innovation by small press publishers.

Most small presses strongly display the fourth criterion, demonstrating a significant tolerance for risk. Paradoxically, it is the limitations of small presses that might ensure their ability to take significant risks. In distinction to traditional publishers, whose significant capitalisation makes it hard to take significant risks in a difficult marketplace, small presses often have low financial investment and no shareholders demanding a responsible use of their capital. In 'Sympathy for the Devil,' Caroline Hamilton notes the peculiar relation to risk of the small press:

> Yet in the globalised, digital era of audience niches, size matters. Small is not just beautiful but has practical business advantages. The usual structures for selling books rarely apply for small independent publishers. They may have no marketing budgets, no automated distribution chains, no advances – and, very commonly, no profits. But, because of this, small presses are also sheltered from the pressures of the market. If a book sells only 25 per cent of its print run, a small press won't take the same hit as a large company that invests hundreds of thousands of dollars in a title. As one small press publisher explained to me, 'If they don't sell a certain number, they're in trouble. For us, it's only a few hundred copies. (Hamilton, 90)

But while small presses may accept a high chance of failure, they risk little in financial terms. Nonetheless, since their risks are often underwritten by their owners, if small publishers fail to recoup their investment, they usually pay the price personally. In large firms, on the other hand, those making the decisions will rarely directly suffer loss. Small presses take risks, not only because the risks are small, but also because they are not responsible to anyone aside from themselves. In a larger organisation, risks cannot be owned in this way and may therefore be avoided. A greater understanding of the risk/reward balance may prove useful to small presses; publishing a work with challenging content may seem like a risk, but, if it isn't backed by adequate marketing and distribution, it may fail to embrace the risky possibility of greater success.

The final criterion is perhaps the one that best describes small press operation. It characterises a social enterprise as an operation which refuses to 'accept a limitation of resources'. Despite real difficulty in securing funding, distribution or extensive readerships, small presses continue to forge forward, working to bring their publications to readers. Small presses operate under difficult conditions, labouring long hours for non-monetary rewards.

Advantages of a Social Entrepreneurship Model

The adoption of an SE model to define non-profit driven, small press publishing would mean redefining the sector by its commitment to benefit a shared culture, rather than by its publications and literary values. The SE model also better captures the value of actions such as publishing experimental work and emerging writers. Because it calculates value in a broad spectrum, an SE model can recognise that supporting emerging writers is necessary for the long-term health of our literary culture. This is true even if we decide that the work published possessed no literary value – though we might hope this is not the case!

Social enterprise is able to calculate value in this broader way, because it defines its goal, its ability to create value, by the delivery of goods to stakeholders (Mort et al. 2003; Dart 2004; Alvord 2004). A stakeholder theory of value is useful in capturing the benefits of a set of actions aside from their monetary value – benefits that in the commercial world might be viewed as either positive or negative externalities. It could be argued that much of the value of small presses lies primarily in the encouragement they give to emerging writers, the space they provide for experimentation and the contribution they make to literary communities, rather than primarily in their dissemination of literary or culturally significant work. Capturing this value allows us better to appreciate the centrality of small presses to our shared culture. Though the language of stakeholder theory may be a novelty in the publishing world, it is well established among public servants and those working for philanthropic organisations. In seeking to attract funding, small presses may be better served speaking of the stakeholder benefits (defined perhaps as writers, editors and the reading public) than basing their justifications on explanations of intrinsic literary value.

Some presses successfully articulate their mission in these terms. Implicitly, if not explicitly, many have identified key stakeholders. *Overland*, for example, has established itself as a voice of the progressive left. Through its online presence, it has proven its ability to shape conversations that go far beyond the journal itself. *Overland*'s overt political orientation lends itself to developing in a recognisably social entrepreneurial way – focused on delivering social goods to key stakeholder groups. It is a lesson, however, that other small presses could benefit from learning.

An SE model would encourage presses to evaluate their work using a wider focus. Rather than viewing their work as solely a matter of producing publications, they might focus also on the contribution they can make to the shared values and goals of their stakeholders. As publishers, in a simplistic sense, our task is simply to produce books – a hugely time-consuming process in and of itself. Small publishers tend to devote their resources, both time and money, to publishing new work. But what if small presses viewed themselves as literary-focused social entrepreneurs? Our task might be to promote new literary voices or to encourage engagement with exciting new literature, or to develop writing that responds to our local context. This might mean that, though the digital or physical book remains central, it becomes just one element in a wider process of cultural engagement.[8]

Once again, many presses do this admirably. *Kill Your Darlings* uses its *Killings* blog, among other initiatives, to engage with readers over and above the content of the journal. It is not only a way of contributing to the community surrounding their journal; it is a way of contributing to our collective literary culture. At Vignette Press, we have tried to do this by running fundraisers and launches that do not limit themselves to touting the publication, but that attempt to foster and celebrate the community around the publication. As fundraisers, our events have yielded modest returns, but as efforts in community building they were highly successful.

---

[8]   This issue of the broadening range of activities by organisations previously thought of as publishers is broached by Overland editor, Jeff Sparrow, in the Winter 2013 edition (Sparrow 2013).

Although the concept of stakeholders is rarely present in current conceptions of publishing, at least at a theoretical level, we would contend that many purchasers of small press books are motivated by a desire to support local culture. Writers, editors and designers also contribute their services for low or no payment to support the small presses that form a vital part of the literary ecosystem. Small presses in turn work hard to further the interests of these stakeholders, by promoting the work of such writers as well as providing opportunities for publication. Nevertheless, a more explicit embrace of the stakeholder concept might help to bind these groups closer to the press – encouraging writers to better understand how their support of small presses is a support of themselves as writers. Readers are also key stakeholders in small presses, and explicitly acknowledging them as such would encourage small presses to engage with readers as part of their core mission. This kind of ongoing communication provides a platform for building a community that goes beyond consumer and supplier.

A significant change in the literary landscape of the past twenty years is the proliferation of creative writing programs. Both these programs, and the students taught by them, constitute significant stakeholders to the work of small press publishers. The programs have been attacked and defended vigorously.[9] As early as 1982, a prominent writing teacher and founder of the Associated Writing Programs, A.W.P. Cassill, called for the organisation to be disbanded and for writers to flee the 'poison' of academia (Menand 2009). But the rise of creative writing programs has not clearly resulted in a parallel rise in sales of the small journals that offer students routes to publication. While the teaching of writing and small press publishing could constitute parts of a tightly integrated cultural ecosystem, they have not worked together as effectively as they might.[10] By conceiving of small presses, creative writing students and their programs as constituting mutual stakeholders in a shared literary culture, an SE model encourages us to find ways of engaging more effectively in shared activities. An SE model makes clear the contribution of small publishers to the creation of vibrant and accessible literary culture over and above their dissemination of writing; the value and relevance of creative writing programs is dependent on the culture nurtured, in part, by small presses. Without a pathway to active engagement, such as publication, creative writing programs are stripped of much of their meaning.

---

[9]   The articles on this subject are endless, but a few more interesting examples include: Batuman (2010), Hall (1983) and Shivani (2010).

[10]   For an interesting counterpoint see Mayr and Read (2011).

A social enterprise model provides a solid foundation for convincing university management outside of arts faculties about the value of building upon these interconnections. Collaboration need not (solely!) take the form of financial support. Greater use of small press titles as set texts would be hugely beneficial. Small press titles might be reviewed as class exercises or small press editors might be used to provide feedback to students. As mentioned, the teaching of creative writing in universities has been the subject of enumerable tirades, rebuttals and apologetics. An effective way to silence the critics of institutionalisation is to show the engagement of universities on the cultural frontlines, and the small press offers one opportunity in which to do this.

Negatives of the Social Entrepreneurship Model

Though social entrepreneurship offers a powerful framework within which to understand certain small press operations, it is not without dangers and limitations. These derive both from the peculiarities of publishing and from the difficulties inherent in SE theory. Before turning to publishing's specific limitations, it is worth examining the strange ideological space SE occupies.

SE functions both as an attempt to resolve social failures engendered by an all-encompassing market and to celebrate the market that created those failures. SE represents, therefore, both a resistance to market thinking and an embrace of it. In this way, SE proponents are made up of both anti-capitalist activists and apologists of laissez-faire neo-liberalism. In a discussion of the social entrepreneurship movement (SEM) and attempts to leverage it to alleviate unemployment, Cook et al. make clear their belief that SE is neo-liberalism's patsy: 'We also conclude that the SEM is indistinguishable from neo-liberalism and as such does not represent a viable solution to unemployment and the welfare needs that accompany it' (Cook et al. 2003, 57). Though one might legitimately decide that the application of SE principles to unemployment represents a very different scenario to its application to small press publishing, there is some justification for viewing SE as tainted by association. These linkages of SE to neo-liberalism can be broken down into three broad categories: theoretical, institutional and political. Theoretically, SE often presupposes the efficiency of the market and the inefficiency of government. Moreover, many commentators define SE in opposition to supposedly inefficient government agencies and traditional not-for-profit organisations.[11]

---

[11] This belief is pervasive in many segments of the literature. Telling examples can be found in: Osborne (1993) and Dees (2007).

Additionally, one of the key drivers of SE adoption is a drive to quantitative, results-driven funding. This in turn necessitates (or at least encourages) the reduction of human, social, cultural and environmental needs to blunt dollar figures. It encourages a mindset that insists that all values are fungible and capable of being readily translated into a common exchange unit: the unit of currency. Obviously, results-driven funding has many strengths. It can enable the delivery of more and better services to those in need. It can reduce waste and uncover illegitimate use of donated funds. But even if we believe result-driven funding is worth adopting, we can still acknowledge how it enforces a market-based viewpoint. Besides any qualms felt about the translation of human values to dollar values, the problem remains that these quantifications are often not determined by a rigorous external mechanism (such as a market). This means that social entrepreneurs may be structurally encouraged to increase secondary quantitatively significant results at the expense of actual results.

The problem is institutional because much of the research being produced on SE emerges from management and business schools. Some proponents wish to widen the category to include shareholder-controlled corporations in this category, where these businesses have expressed social goals to which they aspire (Hemingway 2005). Such goals may sometimes be central to the enterprises mission, but they may also constitute nothing more than marketing or 'greenwashing' – the aspiration extending no further than the company perceives that it can profit from the association.

The ideological skew of SE is political in so far as neo-liberal groups wish to promote SE as an alternative to government-run programs. In the United Kingdom, David Cameron's 'Big Society' is such an attempt to co-opt charity and SE organisations as part of a move to disentangle the government from their obligation to provide public services and a social safety net (Holden et al. 2011; Corbett and Walker 2012). Of course, since SE is frequently defined by its successes (while ignoring its failures), it is efficient and innovative by definition – definitions that explicitly or implicitly are contrasted with the wasteful bureaucracy of government programs. This may or may not be a good thing, but we should, perhaps, be sceptical of the belief that government will continue to provide equal levels of income once they have divested themselves of their responsibility.

More practically, the wholesale adoption of a SE model comes with a substantial theoretical and organisational overhead. Presses taking seriously their status as social entrepreneurs may feel compelled to create detailed mission statements, to gather data on how well they have achieved key goals, to work to connect with stakeholders. Given the small budgets and the time pressures on those involved in publishing, wholeheartedly embracing the model may simply take too much away from the primary purposes of such enterprises – to produce books of value.

Engaging stakeholders also necessitates defining them and appealing to them. There is, perhaps, a systemic tendency to define each stakeholder group as widely as possible, and to define the values which are shared as widely as possible. Literature, on the other hand, has often been thought of as the pursuit of individuals, and it is the individual voice or outlook that is often most valued. This emphasis on individualism has been strongly contested within literary criticism (theoretically by Deconstruction [Naas 2008, 37] and New Historicism [Groden 2012, 373], politically by Marxism [Colebrook 1997, 175] and Feminism [Fox-Genovese 1992]). Nonetheless, practically, there exists a real danger that small presses, if they were to consider themselves as social enterprises, may prioritise work that appeals most strongly to the largest number of stakeholders. The strength of small press publishing often lies in exactly the opposite technique; small presses champion singular voices that may not appeal to a mass readership. Such work may inherently appeal only to a small group or, because working to push back the commonly held aesthetic and cultural preferences, it may appear too difficult. One need not be a rabid individualist to be concerned about the possibility of small presses second-guessing their stakeholders to prioritise the most popular work.

Conclusion

As we have shown, social entrepreneurship is unstable both in its practice and theorisation. In one incarnation, it becomes a way of reclaiming control of market-based thinking and techniques. Defining and using markets as limited but highly useful tools can allow us to achieve genuine, human-focused goals and ideals. On the other hand, SE can be yet another Trojan horse for the encroachment of market-derived thinking into our politics, lives and imaginations. As literature addressing the phenomenon of SE develops, we may be better able to choose those elements that best fit with our deeply held beliefs.

Our examination has suggested to us that SE theory holds significant potential as a way of conceptualising the work of many small press publishers. More importantly, it provides insight into ways that small press organisation can improve their own operations.

If publishers believe that certain readers, editors and writers constitute stakeholders, then they may want to explicitly identify them as such. By explicitly stating a press' driving principles or values, it may encourage stakeholders to identify themselves as a sharing a community of interest. Achieving strong stakeholder communities may necessitate engaging more with these groups, perhaps even the ceding of a certain degree of control; this may very well be the cost of building a strong community. Interaction and social events may not only be important ways increase awareness of authors and publications, but they may also be important ways of pursuing the central goal of supporting a literary community.

The engagement of stakeholders must be balanced with a recognition that small presses require large-scale commitments of time and often money from their publishers, editors and team members. Core members may feel substantially less motivated if they feel they are taking direction from people only peripherally associated with the organisation. The solution, aside from delicate balancing, lies, perhaps, in having an explicit and detailed articulation of mission at the outset. This sets the parameters for those involved and provides them with the assurance that their work will contribute to goals that align with their own values and preferences.

SE also provides a framework in which partnerships can be clearly seen as ways of contributing to common goals. By improving our ability to recognise the value created by small presses outside of disseminating literary work, it may help articulate the value to potential partners of a small publisher. We think this might be particularly fruitful in the relationship of small presses with creative writing departments. Small presses play a significant role in our literary and cultural life. All of those invested in a flourishing literary culture (universities, publishers, booksellers, writers) need to work together to ensure the health of the whole. Working together with small presses need not be a synonym for financial support, but could be an exciting way of leveraging our individual strengths to further literary culture.

Finally, the SE model encourages small press operators to think beyond the printing of books and embrace alternative ways to create value. We are in a time of change with regard to production of books. Digital formats and new printing technologies may be good or bad for the literary world, but they will definitely change how we work and how we read. Embracing innovation and thinking more laterally about how we approach and achieve our goals will help small and independent presses not only survive but also thrive through these difficult and exciting times.

III. Publishing Literature

Chapter 9

IN THE SAME BOAT

Transnationalism, Australian Short Fiction, and the New
Cultural Cringe

Emmett Stinson

Australian literary production has never been an isolated activity confined to national borders. From its inception, Australian literature has always been mediated by a transnational network of publishing and distribution, and the fate of local works of literature has often been profoundly affected by the vicissitudes of the international book trade. Indeed, from the end of the 19th Century until the 1980s, British publishers dominated the Australian book market. Prior to World War Two, their hegemony was so complete that 'it was simpler and more economical for the local trade to organise itself to be importers and retailers rather than publishers with an eye for local literary talent and new forms of literary expression' (Nile and Walker 2001, 8). As Jan Paterson reported, even as late as 1988, London-based publishers still expressed a sense of ownership of the Australian market, saying things like 'Australia is ours', or referring to Australia as 'our traditional market' (ibid., 12).

The economic realities of colonialism were reflected at the level of culture, since authors' hopes for publication and financial success rested in the hands of London publishers or their local representatives. London, quite simply, was the 'production centre for Australian literature' (ibid., 4) and the hegemonic control exerted by British publishers was absolutely a form of a cultural imperialism. As Henry Lawson noted, the result of this situation was that local authors' hopes for broader national recognition absolutely depended upon their ability to gain favourable recognition overseas[1], particularly in London:

---

[1]   More recent research has, however, begun to acknowledge the historical importance of other transnational networks; for one example that examines the relationship between Australian literature and United States publishers, *see* Carter 2010.

> As soon as the Southern writer goes 'home' and gets some recognition in England, he is 'So-and-So, the well-known Australian author whose work has attracted so much attention in London lately; and we first hear of him by cable, even though he might have been writing at his best for ten years in Australia. (Lawson 1984, 426)

In other words, British publishers' control of the Australian book trade was not just economic. They effectively regulated symbolic and social capital within the Australian literary sphere as well, since the few local publishing options that existed struggled to compete meaningfully with overseas houses.

The colonialism of Australian literature also found its socio-psychological corollary in what would become known as the 'cultural cringe', which, as A.A. Phillips pointed out in his seminal 1950 essay, is nothing more than the *internalisation* of Britain's colonial hegemony: 'in the back of the Australian mind, there sits a minatory Englishman ... that Public School Englishman with his detection of a bad smell permanently engraved on his features ... whose indifference to the Commonwealth is not even studied' (Phillips 2012, 84). Britain's material dominion over Australian culture manifested as a mass inferiority complex, a national will to fail that became a self-fulfilling prophecy, stymieing Australia's attempts to forge a national culture.

But Australia, or so we are told, is postcolonial now. Despite many starts and stops, the broader project of Australian cultural nationalism – which was made explicit with the founding of the Australia Council in 1973 – has been underway for decades. Recent public disputes over the alleged 'disappearance' of Australian classics from university classrooms have, ironically, proved that readers' interest in the national literature is as strong as ever. Not only is Australian Literature being 'taught in more than 300 subjects in about 40 tertiary institutions' (Gelder 2012), but also several publishers – including Text, Allen & Unwin and Harper Collins – have begun reprinting classic Australian literary works. As social psychologist Norman Feather demonstrated in the 1990s, Australians are now actually biased *towards* Australian cultural products, rather than suspicious of them. It certainly no longer seems plausible to claim, as Phillips did, that Australians have an internalised upper-class Englishman lurking in their superegos.

As a result, discussions of the cultural cringe are now conducted in the past tense. Cringe-thinking, or so the contemporary narrative goes, can no longer function in a globalised, cosmopolitan, multicultural Australia where local literature circulates in an international milieu. This new literary internationalism is perhaps best exemplified by the designation of Melbourne as an UNESCO City of Literature in the 2008 and the subsequent founding of the Wheeler Centre for Books, Writing and Ideas, but evidence of Australian cultural bodies' increasing collaboration with foreign organisations can be found everywhere: the establishment of the 2012 conference NonfictioNow, which was a joint initiative of RMIT and the University of Iowa's Writers' Workshop; the 2010 creation of if:book Australia, a collaborative venture between the Queensland Writers Centre and the international Institute for the Future of the Book; the 2012 recognition of Clunes as one of sixteen members of the International Organisation of Booktowns; Allen & Unwin's 2010 launch of an Australian version of the Faber Academy, which offers creative writing classes; and the recent announcement of a Melbourne chapter of Alain de Botton's School of Life, which will host literary events, offer 'bibliotherapy', and contain a bookshop run by local seller Readings.

In addition to hosting such major international authors as Jonathan Franzen, Jeffrey Eugenides, Bret Easton Ellis and Margaret Atwood, local literary festivals have sought to bolster their international reach in various ways. In 2012, the Melbourne Writers Festival ran events featuring nearly the entire editorial staff of the *New Yorker*. The Sydney Writers Festival's new director, Jemma Birrell, seems to have been selected largely for her international experience as 'the events director of the legendary Shakespeare and Company bookshop in Paris' (McEvoy 2012). Even literary magazines have gotten into the act. The *Lifted Brow* has published new work from such international authors as Tao Lin, Sam Lipsyte, Sheila Heti, Jim Shepard, Blake Butler and Benjamin Kunkel, and *Higher Arc* magazine appeared at last year's Brooklyn Book Festival. The United States magazine *McSweeney's* recently published an issue dedicated to Australian Aboriginal fiction, and United States actor James Franco wrote the featured story from the 2012 fiction edition of the *Big Issue*. On top of this, large numbers of authors undertake fellowships, grants, exchanges and tertiary study at foreign institutions, and send their work to overseas publishers of books and magazines.

In light of these circumstances, a chorus of authors, critics and pundits have pronounced the cringe dead. Author Susan Johnson argues that, for her sons' generation, 'the cultural cringe has disappeared, and for them questioning the differences between London, New York and Melbourne has no relevance or resonance at all' (Johnson 2010). Ken Gelder and Paul Salzman, in their survey of contemporary Australian literature, *After the Celebration: Australian Fiction 1989–2007* (2009), depict Australia as 'a place that is now seen, not as riven by cultural cringe, but as enabled by cultural incorporation' (Gelder and Salzman 2009, 113). Graham Huggan baldly states that: 'The much agonized-over "cultural cringe" is now considered by most Australians to be an irrelevant issue, although it still resurfaces from time to time in local debates over national core culture' (Huggan 2007, 27).

In what comprises the most emphatic obituary for the cringe, Nick Bryant, in a 2012 *Griffith Review* article, argues that the cringe cannot function in a country that *exports* so many of its cultural producers: 'To use an unlovely phrase heard more commonly in diplomatic and sporting circles, Australia is punching above its weight in the arts and culture' (Bryant 2012, 106). In support of this position, Bryant compiles a long list of various actors and artists who have achieved success overseas.

Have Australians overcome the cultural cringe and learned, as Phillips hoped they would, 'the art of being unselfconsciously ourselves'? While there is a certain truth to some of these claims, I will argue that these eulogies for the cringe typically focus on only one of its forms, ignoring the more complicated nature of Phillips' concept of the cringe – which can manifest in unexpected and paradoxical ways. My suggestion is that the contemporary cultural cringe can only be understood in relation to the transformation of the Australian cultural milieu, which now operates within a diffuse, neo-imperial (or postcolonial), globally networked cultural economy. I think an example of how the cringe currently operates can be found by examining an increasingly marginal – if symbolically important – cultural form: the single-author short story collection.

While the short story may seem an unlikely barometer of cultural change, it is a form that has held a culturally privileged place in Australian letters. The work of short story writers such as Henry Lawson and Barbara Baynton has profoundly shaped how Australia conceives of its national character. Moreover, while the production of novels is still subject to the commercial imperative of profit, single-author short story collections are almost uniformly viewed by publishers as unprofitable. As a result, the fortunes of such collections are profoundly affected by swings in symbolic or cultural capital, and the market for them has accordingly proven far more volatile than for other forms of fiction. These swings in popularity provide a singular insight into how Australians value their literary culture.

The 1970s and '80s saw the rise of a 'new wave' of Australian short story writers – Murray Bail, Helen Garner, Peter Carey, Frank Moorhouse and Robert Drewe, among many others – who revitalised the form. If this was the apex of the Australian short story's cultural influence, as is commonly accepted, then the early 2000s were its nadir. From 2000 to 2006, single-author short story collections virtually disappeared from the Australian literary marketplace, unless, as Gelder and Salzman noted, they were written by 'novelists with high public profiles and (one assumes) guaranteed sales' (Gelder and Salzman, 97). Indeed, most of the notable short story collections produced in this period – Tim Winton's *The Turning* (2004), Gillian Mears's *A Map of Gardens* (2002), Mandy Sayer's *15 Kinds of Desire* (2001) and Eva Hornung's *Majar* (2003) – were written by relatively established authors who had already published novels and had either won or been shortlisted for major literary awards. Emerging authors who concentrated on short fiction could not expect to publish their work in book form, even if they had published extensively in magazines and had won multiple prizes.

From the perspective of 2013, this situation seems unimaginable. There has been such a resurgence of the form over the last six years or so, that one can almost speak of a *glut* of short story collections – including books by such authors as Ryan O'Neill, Amanda Lohrey, Tim Richards, Paddy O'Reilly, Josephine Rowe, Jennifer Mills, Paul Mitchell, Patrick Holland, Tom Cho, Jess Huon, Patrick Cullen, Steven Amsterdam, Tony Birch, Chris Somerville, James Roy, Amanda Curtin, A.S. Patric, Wayne Macauley, Anson Cameron, Andy Kissane, Catherine Harris, Cameron Raynes, Janette Turner Hospital, and many others. Another ten single-authored volumes have been produced by two sustained attempts to revive the popularity of short story collections. The first of these, Affirm Press's 'Long Story Shorts' series, was started in 2010 and produced six single-authored collections (including my own) over about 18 months. The second, the creation of the publisher Spineless Wonders, has so far produced four works by single authors and two anthologies. Many of these are the work of debut authors. It is worth noting, however, that virtually all of these books have been produced by small and mid-sized independent publishers, rather than large, multinational corporations.

As book reviewer Jo Case noted in 2010, this renaissance of short fiction publishing can be attributed to the publication of two breakout collections:

> Short stories are newly fashionable in Australian publishing. Arguably, it began with the success of Cate Kennedy's *Dark Roots* in 2006, proving it was possible to become a household name on the back of stories – and paving the way for Nam Le's international bestseller, *The Boat*, two years later. This year has seen a comparative flood in locally published collections. (Case 2010, 29)

It is worth emphasising that many of these subsequent works were written *before* the publication of Le's and Kennedy's stories, and thus the current 'glut' represents a backlog of work that had been previously deemed commercially unviable. Wayne Macauley's *Other Stories* (2010), for example, includes many stories more than a decade old and one that dates back to 1993. Nevertheless, within the publishing industry, there is a sense that Le's and Kennedy's collections marked a turning point for Australian short fiction.

But how did Le's and Kennedy's collections break through publishers' and readers' general lack of interest in short fiction in the early twenty first century? And why do these two collections continue to hold a privileged place, despite the appearance of dozens of other short story collections over the last several years? Why have these been deemed the 'best' examples of the contemporary Australian short story? In a sense, the success of these books is somewhat surprising. Though both Le's and Kennedy's stories are well-wrought, displaying all of the careful craft that institutionalised forms of creative writing aspire to, there is something deeply conservative about the aesthetics of both books, which seem happy to work within the confines of well-established traditions, rather than trying to expand or exceed them. Both may have been breakout successes, but there is little about either work that can be considered legitimately groundbreaking. I want to suggest, instead, that the Australian reception of Le's and Kennedy's books – as reflected in both reviews and profile pieces – was profoundly and positively influenced by overseas responses to their work. My point here is that, whatever one thinks of their literary merit, both the material success of these books and the effusive critical praise that has been heaped upon them have been dramatically influenced by their international reception.

On the face of it, this claim may seem dubious in Kennedy's case. Prior to the publication of *Dark Roots*, she had established herself as a prominent Australian short story writer by winning a variety of regional and national competitions, including the *Age* Short Story Award in consecutive years (2000 and 2001) – a fact often noted in reviews. This, in and of itself, is interesting, in that it testifies to the increasing role that literary prizes of various kinds play in affecting the reception of authors, though a full consideration of this trend is beyond the scope of this essay. She had also published three books of poetry and a memoir, although none of these works received anything like the broader recognition that would accompany the publication of her first book of short stories. Indeed, the turning point for Kennedy's Australian reception came when – just prior to the release of *Dark Roots* – she had a story, 'Black Ice', published in the *New Yorker*.

After the publication of her story in this prestigious overseas magazine, Kennedy was no longer simply a promising Australian author, but an internationally recognised one. This fact was seized upon by the media when her book was released. Nowhere is this better articulated than in a profile of Kennedy from 16 September 2006 written by Jane Sullivan:

> This year is surely the time and place for Kennedy, who is possibly the most successful short-fiction writer in Australia, if you judge success by prizes and places in anthologies. But it's taken 14 years of steady writing to reach the point where she can see her fiction in the *New Yorker* and in her own book: her first short story collection, *Dark Roots*. (Sullivan 2006)

It's notable that the *New Yorker* gets top billing here, and Kennedy's book is mentioned almost as an afterthought. The implication – and it is repeated across virtually all of the media around Kennedy's book – is clear. Local accolades are all well and good, but publication in the *New Yorker* sits on another level. As Frank Moorhouse once quipped, *Meanjin* is an Aboriginal word meaning 'rejected from the *New Yorker*'.

Six years later, in a 2012 interview with the Wheeler Centre, Kennedy was asked to name 'the most significant moment in [her] writing career' (Kennedy 2012). Perhaps inevitably, she listed publication in the *New Yorker* as her defining achievement: 'it hit me that an editor at the *New Yorker* was sitting up at 10.30 at night their time, devoting time to a story of mine, and soon it would be in the actual magazine … the shock came home to me then. Literally [*sic*]' (ibid.). Kennedy's excitement is, on one level, understandable; on another level, there is something depressing about the fact that Kennedy views the publication of a *single story* in a United States magazine as being more important than any of the five books she has published or the many Australian awards she has won. Would an American or English author of Kennedy's stature view publication in the *New Yorker* in the same way?

If Kennedy's comparatively modest success overseas (and let's remember that the *New Yorker* publishes fiction in all of its 47 annual issues) could so drastically affect her Australian reception, it is hardly surprising that Nam Le's multiple overseas successes were prominently mentioned in virtually every Australian review of *The Boat*. James Ley addresses the issue in the first sentence of his *Age* review, noting that Le 'lives in the United States where he has attended the prestigious Iowa Writers' Workshop' (Ley 2008). Nathanael O'Reilly's review for *Antipodes* frames Le's book in similar terms: '*The Boat*, Nam Le's remarkable debut collection of stories, has deservedly garnered a plethora of glowing reviews from around the globe for the young Vietnamese-Australian author' (O'Reilly 2009, 93). A 2009 profile in *The Age* opens by listing all of Le's overseas accolades, as if summarising his *curriculum vitae*:

> At just 30, Vietnam-born, Melbourne-raised writer Nam Le has been blessed with early success. *The Boat*, his debut collection of short stories, was published last year to a wave of international critical acclaim. In addition, Le has been awarded several major awards, including the Dylan Thomas Prize – the richest in Britain. Furthermore, he is the fiction editor of the *Harvard Review*. (Tacon 2009)

It's worth emphasising the force that this kind of framing exerts on Australian reviews. Overseas success immediately increases the visibility of Australian books. Most short story collections are lucky to receive lengthy reviews in *any* major news outlet; *The Boat* received extended reviews in virtually every Australian publication that normally reviews books and many that don't. Moreover, foreign accolades – especially in the case of Le, who had already been reviewed favourably *twice* in the *New York Times* – almost inevitably lead to glowing Australian notices. Any reviewer offering a negative assessment of *The Boat* would effectively be questioning the legitimacy of such august overseas institutions as the Iowa Writers' Workshop, Harvard University, and the *New York Times*.

The Australian reception of *The Boat* was almost unanimous in its glowing praise – an extremely unusual state of affairs. One of the few reviewers to offer even faint criticism of Le's work was James Ley, who, despite offering a favourable assessment of *The Boat*, noted that Le's stories are 'polished to a point where any barb of originality has been sanded away' (Ley). It is interesting to contrast Le's reception with Kennedy's in this instance. Although Kennedy had received many prizes within Australia, her overseas reputation was not as well established and reviews of her work in Australia were far more varied. Although *Dark Roots* has taken on the status of a contemporary classic, many reviewers were openly critical of her work.

Delia Falconer's review in the *Australian Book Review*, for example, ended by noting that 'While Kennedy's stories pay brief, clear-eyed attention to ordinary moments of potential poetry, they seem, taken together, to be missing the messiness, verve and veering joy that are part of life' (Falconer 2006, 50).

Reviews of Le's work also differed in that they explicitly foregrounded a set of biographical details that made him an exemplary representative of contemporary Australia. The first line of the *Sydney Morning Herald*'s review of *The Boat* makes this clear: 'Nam Le was born in Vietnam, grew up in Melbourne and is making a name for himself in the US' (Reimer 2008). Almost every review of *The Boat* refers to Le's multiple nationalities, positioning him as a representative of a cosmopolitan, multicultural and globalised Australia. Of course, there are good textual imperatives for reviewers to mention these issues, not only because *The Boat* explicitly sets its stories in various locations around the globe, but also because Le both makes explicit and ironises his own position in the collection's now famous opening story, 'Love and Honour and Pity and Pride and Compassion and Sacrifice', which features an Australian writer named Nam Le who is studying at the University of Iowa and is nervous about being pegged as an author of so-called 'Ethnic Literature'.

But the fact that Le self-reflexively ironises his position does not change it. And in many ways, Le's deft use of self-deprecating humour draws attention away from the reality of the very strange space he occupies as a cultural figure. I make no claim here to know anything about Le as a person; I am commenting only on his public persona. On the one hand, he is an exemplar of a transnational, cosmopolitan creative class that seems to transgress traditional national, ethnic and racial categories. On the other hand, Le is a figure of the establishment, whose achievements have been consecrated and authorised by a series of elite international institutions that possess significant stores of symbolic capital, such as the University of Iowa, Harvard, and the *New York Times*. Le, at least as a cultural figure, is able to have it both ways, simultaneously representing the margin and the centre, the local and the global, the new transnational creative class and the traditional institutional centres of symbolic capital, by combining his ambition with an ironic self-effacement that seems quintessentially Australian.

The paradoxical cultural position that Le occupies demonstrates how the contemporary cultural cringe operates. In its current form, the cringe does not mean that Australians openly disparage their own culture, but rather that more value and prestige attaches to those Australian cultural products which have been validated by well-respected overseas institutions with high reserves of symbolic capital. Put simply, a book that has overseas impact (to use the fashionable academic term) means more than a book that has a purely local impact. This is the form of the new cringe.

Tracing the shape of this new cringe, however, requires grasping that Phillips' conception of the cringe is more complicated than usually acknowledged. At the heart of the cringe was an anxiety about the quality of Australian culture in relation to foreign culture, which most commonly manifested as a suspicion of local works. But as Phillips pointed out, there were a variety of different strategies for coping with this anxiety, including, for example, extreme displays of nationalism, which he termed the 'Cringe Inverted', a tendency associated with 'the God's-Own-country-and-I'm-a-better-man-than-you-are Australian bore' (Phillips 81). The cringe, according to Phillips' account, is a condition that produces both nationalists and Anglophiles. The cringe's essential character does not lay in its specific manifestation, but rather in this anxiety about Australian culture – an anxiety that is typically *unconscious* – which results 'in a tendency to make needless comparisons' (ibid., 81) between local and international culture.

The new internationalism repeats the anxiety at the heart of the cringe precisely because of its desire to demonstrate, as Nick Bryant attempted to argue, that 'Australia is punching above its weight in the arts and culture'. In this sense, Bryant's article, which highlights the overseas success of contemporary Australian artists, is actually a product of the contemporary cultural cringe that seeks to value Australian cultural products in the mirror of a global marketplace. This desire to situate Australian culture in a global context is another coping strategy for combating the nervousness about Australian culture. And the result, as current Emerging Writers Festival director Sam Twyford-Moore noted in an article for the *Los Angeles Review of Books*, is that young Australian writers are going overseas:

> ... to, effectively, legitimize their practice. An artist friend of mine said that he was getting calls from galleries and curators only once his plane took off from Sydney en route to Berlin – that he had somehow showed some extra commitment by relocating, even though his work had not necessarily changed in shape nor form. (Twyford-Moore 2012)

One of the cultural cringe's defining features, according to Phillips, was that Australians did not trust their own aesthetic judgment. The new cringe continues this pattern by relying on international reception (particularly in

Western, English-speaking countries) to consecrate Australian artists – a tendency that Henry Lawson observed a century ago.

From my perspective, the new cringe's internationalism perpetuates what Sylvia Lawson termed 'the paradox of being colonial' in *The Archibald Paradox* (1983). For Lawson, this paradox – which is constitutive of both Australian nationalism and the kind of thinking that resulted in the cringe – comprises a dual imperative to 'know enough of the metropolitan world' to 'move and think internationally', while resisting internationalism 'strongly enough for the colony to cease to be colonial and become its own place' (Lawson 1983, xvi). In other words, the paradox of being colonial combines a cosmopolitan sensibility, on the one hand, with a strident nationalism, on the other. While the new internationalism may take a slightly different form, it still results from a complicated – and often paradoxical – combination of nationalism and cosmopolitanism. I would argue, for example, that Nam Le has been so readily adopted as a figure of literary nationalism *precisely because* he is an international figure, who is both local *and* foreign, cosmopolitan but still recognisably Australian, as evidenced in both his self-deprecating humour and his note-perfect imitation of Tim Winton in 'Halflead Bay'. Here Australia's perception of itself as a globally aware, cosmopolitan nation paradoxically forms the grounds of a new discourse of Australian nationalism. Indeed, as Ghassan Hage has argued, the 'cosmopolite' is the 'new dominant figure in the history of Australian nationalism' (Hage 2000, 201).[2]

It is worth emphasising that I am not raising these concerns about the new literary internationalism in order to reassert the importance of establishing an institutionalised and consecrated canon of national literature, as some have recently done.[3] From my perspective, such literary nationalism is undesirable for two reasons: not only does it foster a conservative, unnuanced and decontextualised approach to literature that is ultimately ahistorical, but also, for the reasons I have outlined above, such nationalist positions actually serve to reinforce the anxieties that underpin the cringe. Nor do I see this new cringe as some sort of 'decline' in cultural standards that

---

[2]   See Hage 2000, 201. See also, Hage, 204: See also, Hage, 204: 'White multiculturalism raises the crucial question: who has the competence to enjoy ethnic cultural diversity? The very language of White multiculturalism (diversity, difference, etc.) presupposes a "cultured" and sublimated approach to otherness devoid of a too materialist functionality, which the upper classes use to distinguish themselves and exclude the less "cultured" people.'

[3]   See, for example, Williamson 2012.

represents a fall from a golden age of literary production. In point of fact, I see the new cringe as perpetuating an older set of anxieties, albeit in a novel permutation.

My concern with the new cringe lies in its potential to result in a levelling of culture. Here, the *style* of both Le's and Kennedy's work is crucial. Both are practitioners of an over-refined style of writing that, for better or worse, has traditionally been associated with United States creative writing programs.[4] While I don't mean this as quite the value judgment that it might appear to be, I think it is both accurate and fair to describe Le's and Kennedy's work as part of what is effectively a contemporary academicism (which I mean in the sense of academic painting) that privileges a certain kind of 'polished' writing, and which seeks to present a smooth and unbroken illusion of presence. While such writing may take up one set of Modernist literary techniques (such as parataxis, the objective correlative, the epiphany), it avoids those techniques frequently associated with the avant-garde (such as metonymy, intellectual montage, artificial constraint and other conceptual approaches), which would threaten to undermine this carefully constructed impression of textual unity. Rather than aiming for aesthetic originality, novelty, shock, or defamiliarisation, this contemporary academicism seeks to reproduce or refine its specific style, which is ultimately an ahistorical simulacrum derived from a selective and simplistic reading of a much more complicated and fraught literary tradition.

Kennedy's writing tends towards minimal realism, while Le's writing self-consciously inhabits a series of different genres (a fact that is ironically noted in *The Boat*, in which it is stated that the fictional Nam Le prefers 'to write about lesbian vampires and Colombian assassins, and Hiroshima orphans – and New York painters with haemorrhoids') (Le 2008, 9). But both authors approach their work from within the framework of this academicism. Le has frequently been praised – by Michiko Kakutani, among others – for his 'ventriloquism' (Kakutani 2008), his ability to *emulate* other styles, although Le has, again, ironised this descriptor in a self-effacing and sarcastic talk called 'On Ventriloquism'. But while his ventriloquism is impressive, Le's stories often feel like a set of genre exercises that precisely

---

4   It's worth acknowledging that the actual output of creative writing programs is, of course, considerably more varied than such generalisations typically acknowledge. However, in this instance, I am arguing that Le and Kennedy's stylistic approaches draw on precisely the traditions that are typically associated with United States creative writing programs in particular. For a more nuanced account of the diversity of writing that has been produced by creative writing programs, see McGurl 2009.

imitate their sources without transcending them (I once heard an offhand critique of *The Boat* that more or less sums up its flaws in one line: 'that book is the work of an A student'). Kennedy's work fits even more explicitly into a tradition of United States minimalist realism, whose avatars are writers like Ernest Hemingway, Raymond Carver and Grace Paley. In her review of *Dark Roots*, Delia Falconer notes the influence of these academic conceptions of creative writing on Kennedy's work, suggesting that she has 'an almost American sensibility' even if she 'avoids the length of exposition that distinguishes much of the contemporary short fiction coming out of places such as the Iowa Writers' Workshop' (Falconer, 50). In both cases, the authors display a scholastic and ultimately uncritical reverence for this tradition. While their writing is possessed of an undeniable skill and artisanship, their stories – however beautifully crafted – rarely rise above pastiche.

The dominance of this new academicism – which threatens to become *the* international style of short fiction writing – is occurring at precisely the moment when writers with other kinds of aesthetic goals are struggling to find readers. Giramondo publisher, Ivor Indyk, recently raised precisely this question: 'How much more difficult is it then for young writers working in an expressive or poetic mode, especially when they are writing from traditions that place a high value on richness of voice and the embellishments of metaphor?' (Indyk 2012) Such authors will face increasing difficulty in a literary marketplace that expects fiction to be made to specification, so that it can be exported as easily as Ikea flat-packed furniture. Writers increasingly face two equally unappealing choices: they must either conform to the international style in the hope of accessing a broader readership, or else remain true to their aesthetic convictions and risk relegating their work to obscurity.

One of the virtues, or so it seems to me, of the 'new wave' of short story writing in Australia during the 1970s and '80s was that it reflected the interests of a new generation of readers, resulting in stories that were formally experimental while representing an increasing diversity of viewpoints and speaking positions (Hegenhan 1986, xxi).[5] While I do not

---

[5] In point of fact, Michael Wilding actually voiced similar concerns about the effects of literary internationalisation during the 1970s. See Wilding 1978, 308: '"Internationalism" means having the product of the economically dominant imperialist aggressor thrust onto the market of the second or third world consumer; literature is as much a product as any other manufactured commodity, and it bears an ideological message as part of its identity.'

want to fall into a trap of lionising a specific period in history and am well aware that the past is no panacea, it strikes me that a comparison between the two 'waves' of short fiction raises some essential questions: What if Australia's cultural transnationalism and cosmopolitanism results not in a new diversity, but a new homogenisation? What if measuring Australian writing in the mirror of global culture means that we only get back a reflection of *other* already-established traditions? And what if books that don't adhere to the specifications of an approved style face the prospect of being ignored by audiences altogether, resulting in what Wyndham Lewis once described as the 'discouragement of too much unconservative originality'? (Lewis 1930, 123).

Chapter 10

TWITTER, LITERARY PRIZES AND THE CIRCULATION OF CAPITAL

Beth Driscoll

Among the rapid changes that characterise publishing in the twenty-first century, a number of phenomena are increasingly influential. Two of these are literary prizes and social media, both of which draw together participants from multiple areas of literary culture. Their intersection depicts with unusual clarity some of the dynamics of the contemporary literary field.

This paper presents a case study of the Twitter conversation about the 2012 Prime Minister's Literary Awards in Australia, which was organised by the hashtag #PMAwards. The collected data shows a wide range of Twitter users commenting on the prize, but only over a short period and only at the quite simple level of reporting news or offering congratulations. However, this ephemeral and perhaps superficial conversation performs important work. Drawing on the theoretical model of Pierre Bourdieu, this paper argues that the exchanges of information and personal messages that took place during the discussion of the 2012 Prime Minister's Literary Awards facilitated conversion between forms of capital, transforming the symbolic capital and media capital of the prize into social capital for Twitter users. The case study suggests that literary awards and Twitter help build networks of recognition and influence among agents in the literary field.

Social Media and the Literary Field

In the past few years, developing a social media strategy and a presence on social networks such as Twitter has become almost mandatory for publishers. Even three years ago, this wasn't necessarily the case. A *Publishers Weekly* article in 2010 suggested that Twitter was embraced more by independent publishers than the big houses, and was predominantly viewed as 'more of a time-suck than anything else' (Deahl 2010). However, by 2012 a *Publishers*

Weekly survey listed 198 publishers' Twitter accounts, indicating extensive adoption across the industry (Habash 2012). Some of these Twitter accounts have only small groups of followers: the electronics and engineering publisher Newnes Press, for example, has 160 (ibid.). Other publishers have very significant numbers of people who read their tweets. In 2012, Lonely Planet had the largest number of followers at 800,000 (ibid.): as I write this, the number of followers has risen to 985,282. There is a widespread sense that Twitter provides important potential business opportunities for publishers. 'Hand-selling' books on the internet through social media was recently named as one of the 'Ten Ways to Save Publishing' by publisher Colin Robinson in *The Guardian* (2012).

However, while many publishers have embraced Twitter, its economic value and the models of best practice for its use are still somewhat unknown. A number of guides promise to help the publishing industry maximise the benefits of social networking: see, for example, *10 Practical Twitter Tips for Publishers* (Sherk 2010), *The Publishing Talk Guide to Twitter* (Reed 2011) and *Book Marketing Basics; How to use Facebook, Twitter, Blogging and Email Marketing to Connect with Readers* (Duolit 2012). Despite the marketing emphasis of these titles, the tenor of the advice in all of them is that Twitter is not a bare promotional tool. Rather, it functions most effectively as a form of engagement with other users: it requires the social. As Adam Sherk writes, 'No one likes the guy at the party who does nothing but talk about himself. Be sure to share things from other sources too and get involved in related conversations' (2010). Similarly, Rachel Deahl observes in *Publishers Weekly* that 'the sales approach is one thing that doesn't work … on Twitter it's extremely important to be genuine … the key is talking to people – not at them' (Deahl 2010). Deahl interviews literary agent Colleen Lindsay, who notes that the best Twitter users are often editors rather than marketers because they create 'new ways to connect not only with potential readers but with writers and agents as well' (ibid.). That is, Twitter works most effectively when users create bonds with one another that go beyond simple commercial transactions.

Twitter's format makes these ties observable: users can see who follows a publisher, who retweets (forwards) their comments, and who replies to them. Such connections, explicit and traceable, produce a visible expression of community. In this, Twitter is an embodiment of Bourdieu's field theory. Bourdieu defines fields as sociological mappings that depict 'social microcosms, separate and autonomous spaces' that are also networks of 'objective relations' (domination or subordination, complementarity or antagonism) between positions (1996, 181, 231). The field is a force field, subject to pressures, as well as a game or war field, a site where strategies are deployed in a competitive struggle (ibid., 232). Society is made up of numerous fields, including the field of economics and the field of politics as well as the field of cultural production and its subset, the literary field. The literary field comprises agents and institutions involved in the creation and reception of literature and their behaviours. Twitter offers a glimpse into the twenty-first century manifestation of this field. It shows the objective relations and interactions between a wide range of agents – publishers, readers, libraries and so on – inflected by the workings of a globally mobilised market and highly developed technological capabilities.

One of the chief activities of the literary field is the exchange of different forms of capital. Capital is most commonly appreciated as an economic asset, but is widely recognised as having other forms. In his seminal essay, *The Forms of Capital*, Bourdieu describes a schema according to which capital is presented in three guises: economic, cultural and social (2007 [1986], 84). He posits that economic capital is the root of all other types, but that these 'transformed, disguised' forms of capital are never entirely reducible to economic capital, and can in fact produce their effects by concealing their basis in economic capital (ibid., 91). Bourdieu defines social capital as 'the aggregate of actual or potential resources which are linked to a possession of a durable network of more or less institutionalised relationships of mutual acquaintance and recognition' (ibid., 88). Thus, the volume of social capital an agent possesses depends on the number of connections he or she can mobilise, and the amount of economic, cultural and social capital possessed by each of those connections (ibid., 89). The existence of a network of connections is not a natural or social given, but is acquired through acts of socialisation 'in which recognition is endlessly affirmed and reaffirmed', so that short-term acquaintances become durable relationships (ibid., 90).

Twitter is a key tool for the acquisition of social capital in the twenty-first century. It enables acts of recognition that can potentially transform acquaintances into durable (albeit remote) relationships. On Twitter, acts of socialisation are instances of communication, requiring content. Ties are made through exchanges of messages, and this is where social media and literary prizes connect.

Literary Prizes and the Circulation of Capital

Prizes are prominent providers of literary news. They are increasingly numerous, with over 50 major literary awards in Australia and hundreds more internationally. In addition, they are recurring features of the literary calendar, forming a regular news cycle: the Miles Franklin Award in June, the Man Booker Prize in October, and so on. Prizes provide multiple, regular spikes of interest for the literary field.

Prizes possess media power. Their narrative framework of entries, shortlist and winner is comprehensible to a broad public, making prizes readily translatable into news stories. Prizes are also inherently provocative due to their claims to anoint the 'best' works. This invites multiple media reports that spotlight and develop controversies over which books should be consecrated. These controversies spill over into all aspects of a prize's operation, from judges who resign (Sedgmann 2004), to the dearth of women winning major awards (Coslovich 2011), to the axing of prizes on political grounds (Megalogenis 2012). Their structural features of competition and consecration make prizes extremely media-friendly, and this plays out across social networks as well as the mainstream media.

The media power of prizes is an asset, a form of capital. Nick Couldry uses the term 'media meta-capital' to denote the ability of the media to 'exercise power over other forms of power' (2003, 667). According to Couldry, one of the key features of media meta-capital is that it is easily convertible into other forms of capital: 'media-based symbolic capital developed in one field can under certain conditions be directly exchanged for symbolic capital in another field' (ibid., 669). He gives as an example a well-known British television gardener who then became a successful popular novelist (ibid.).

The media meta-capital of literary prizes has significant impacts on the literary field. Crucially, through their own visibility, prizes provide associated agents with media-based capital that they can use in a variety of ways. Winners of literary awards can use media meta-capital to convert their symbolic capital as writers into the economic capital of increased sales, speaking opportunities or licensing deals. Commercial sponsors of literary awards can use the media meta-capital generated by the prize to turn their economic capital into increased prestige or goodwill. In this article, I look at another kind of transformation effected through media meta-capital: the transformation of a prize's symbolic capital into social capital for Twitter users. This process is illustrated by an extended case study of the way in which one prize was discussed on Twitter in 2012.

Case Study: The Prime Minister's Literary Awards 2012

The Prime Minister's Literary Awards are relatively recent, inaugurated in 2008, but are gaining a place among the most significant Australian literary prizes. They offer prizes in several categories including fiction, non-fiction, children's books, young adult fiction, poetry and history, and are the richest literary awards in Australia, currently giving $80,000 to each winner. The fiction award is broadly framed, with no limitation equivalent to the Miles Franklin Award's requirement that works 'portray Australian life'. From its origin, several structural features of the prize have been geared towards popular promotion. There is a significant budget allocated to publicity, an email list keeps interested parties informed about prize developments, and in 2012 an official hashtag was set up to encourage Twitter conversations about the prize.

In its short history, the Prime Minister's Literary Awards have accrued and bestowed many different forms of capital: the symbolic capital developed through consecrating a series of writers; the economic capital generated through cash grants, augmented sales and increased visibility for the book industry; as well as media meta-capital through the prize's coverage in the media. Analysing the Twitter conversation about the Prime Minister's Literary Awards in 2012 gives some indication of how these forms of capital are converted into social capital by Twitter users.

For this research, I used the free, web-based program Netlytic (www.netlytic.org) to collect and analyse tweets. Netlytic has been used elsewhere to analyse social networks related to cultural practices. For example, Anatoliy Gruzd and DeNel Rehberg Sedo used the software to analyse reading practices among the *1 book 1 Twitter* digital book club (2012), while Jennifer Grek Martin has used Netlytic to study the online community, TheOneRing.net, which brings together fans of *The Lord of the Rings* (2011).

My study collected all tweets identified with the hashtag #PMAwards made over a period of a single month in 2012, starting a few days before the announcement of the winner on 17 July and continuing until 17 August. By limiting the study to those tweets that used the official hashtag, I missed many tweets that were on this topic but did not use the hashtag, either accidentally or deliberately. The advantage of the more contained study is that it ensures a high proportion of relevant data, since only a few tweets using this hashtag appear to be spam. Further, framing the case study using the official hashtag enables analysis of the emerging practice of designating Twitter tags to organise social media discussions of literary prizes: The Man Booker Prize and the Victorian Premier's Literary Awards also set up official hashtags in 2012.

My research gathered 622 tweets. While this is not a very large set, it nonetheless has significance. At one point #PMAwards was among the most actively used hashtags in Sydney and Melbourne. The company Trendsmap, which tweets as TrendsSydney and TrendsMelbourne (in addition to other accounts) tracks popular tweeted words and identified #PMAwards as trending in both cities on the morning of the announcement:

23/07/12 10:43   TrendsSydney   #pmawards is now trending in #Sydney http://t.co/mFyNaFiv
23/07/12 11:20   TrendsMelbourne   #pmawards is now trending in #Melbourne http://t.co/
                                                     NPVfdHKR

'Trending' as used by Trendsmap is not objectively defined by numbers of tweets, but assessed as a relative spike of popularity compared to other words; it is a measure that records sudden increases in tweeting activity. The status of #PMAwards as a trending topic indicates that the prize had an impact on Twitter, at least in metropolitan Australia.

The set of 622 tweets produced by this study can be analysed across a range of axes. The following sections use the data to address some key questions: who were the active tweeters, when were most people tweeting, and what kinds of things did they write about the Prime Minister's Literary Awards? Such information gives insight into how media, symbolic and social capital circulated in the literary field through this Twitter event.

The field of participants

The total set of 622 tweets was spread among 343 individual posters. This indicates that quite a lot of people participated in this virtual event, but that many of these people posted only once. The ten most frequent commenters accounted for 122 tweets, about 20 per cent of the total, a relatively low proportion that further demonstrates a broad conversation. The pie chart below identifies the top ten posters using the #PMAwards hashtag, many of whom contributed a roughly equal amount:

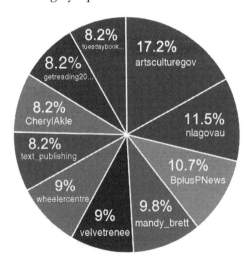

This data suggests that the impetus and enthusiasm for this event was not unilaterally driven, but shared among the field of Twitter users who used the #PMAwards hashtag.

We can sketch this field in more detail by looking more closely at the identities of these top posters. They represent a large variety of players in the publishing industry, and include both institutions and individuals. The most prolific poster, artsculturegov, is the Twitter feed for Arts and Culture from the Australian Government's Office for the Arts, the federal department responsible for administering the prize. Its active tweeting shows a leadership role in initiating and maintaining media coverage. Another government body that tweeted prolifically was Get Reading (getreading2012). Previously known as Books Alive, this is an annual government initiative aimed at stimulating the book industry. Its Twitter account was an important component of its strategy to raise the visibility of books in Australia in 2012, and it participated in a number of Twitter conversations about books and reading. Get Reading's director, Cheryl Akle (CherylAkle), also appears on this chart as she tweeted about the prize from her personal account.

Another active group of posters in this discussion was libraries. The National Library of Australia (nlagovau) hosted the prize ceremony and follow-up events. It is an active Twitter user, having posted over 2500 tweets and accumulated 8500 followers. A number of libraries have embraced digital networks and social media, and many participated to some extent in discussion of the Prime Minister's Literary Awards. These include Ashfield Library, Stanton Library and Hills Library in Sydney and the Athenaeum Library in Melbourne, which tweeted:

23/07/12 11:26 LibraryAthena Congratulations all the winners of the #PMawards! Why not drop into the Ath and pick up one to read?

BplusPNews, the Twitter account for industry publication *Bookseller and Publisher*, was also among the top ten participants: Twitter is a key component of *Bookseller and Publisher's* diversified media presence, which also includes a print magazine, email newsletter and website. Another media outlet represented in the list include the ABC television show *First Tuesday Book Club* (tuesdaybookclub); ABC Radio National program *Books and Arts* also had a strong presence. The status of literary awards as media spectacles makes this high participation by media organisations a natural fit: literary journalism is closely linked to the prize cycle.

Individuals such as Mandy Brett (mandy_brett) and Renee Senogles (velvetrenee) appear in this top ten through their personal Twitter accounts, although these people also have professional roles within the literary field: Brett is an editor at Text Publishing, and Senogles is a book publicist and on the staff of the Sydney Writers' Festival. Another top ten participant, The Wheeler Centre, has become a highly influential literary hub in Melbourne and pursues this through a vibrant Twitter presence: its account has 8500 tweets and nearly 13,500 followers.

The only publisher to make the list of top tweeters is Text Publishing, a very active Twitter user with over 11,000 tweets and 7000 followers. Other publishers participated in this conversation to a lesser extent, including three publishers of winning titles, Allen and Unwin (who have 6205 followers), Melbourne University Publishing (954 followers) and Penguin Books Australia (21,304 followers). While no booksellers appear in the top ten users, many of them joined in this Twitter conversation, including Dymocks Adelaide, Abbey Bookshop and Shearers Bookshop in Sydney, and the Australian-based online seller Booktopia.

This diverse list of commenters – encompassing government, publishing professionals, libraries, media outlets, publishers and booksellers – shows that the conversation about the Prime Minister's Literary Awards incorporated a broad cross-section of the literary field. However, to understand the dynamics of this social network it is important to realise that its participants are objectively related to one another in an asymmetrical power structure.

Not all Twitter users enjoy the same status, or possess equivalent amounts of capital. Twitter is a noticeably hierarchical space. Gruzd and Sedo note that Twitter is unlike Facebook in that connections between Twitter users are often not reciprocal and 'this often leads to the creation of power users who have many more followers than the number of people they follow back; power is thus put in the hands of a few influential users' (2012, 3). Power users are more widely followed and their comments more retweeted, allowing them to accumulate a large amount of media and social capital. The power relations at work in the #PMAwards conversation are evidenced in the figure below showing the posters who were most often mentioned by others, including through direct replies or retweets. Mentions increase the visibility and reach of a user, and thus are a measure of these users' influence.

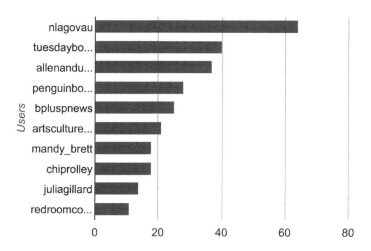

We see here a similar spread among types of people and institutions, although there are some notable differences in the users themselves. The two most mentioned users were the National Library of Australia (nlagovau) and *First Tuesday Book Club* (tuesdaybook). Both users were at the prize ceremony itself – indeed, the National Library was the host – and they provided up-to-the-minute 'live tweeting' which was highly valued and circulated in the Twitter conversation. Some of the National Library of Australia's tweets are:

20/07/12 14:30	Nlagovau	We'll be live tweeting from the #PMAwards at @nlagovau next Mon 23 July, 9am-1pm. See this year's finalists here: http://t.co/8iqvnRJB
23/07/12 9:43	Nlagovau	PM Julia Gillard speaking at the #PMAwards http://t.co/4ANuyRgw
23/07/12 9:57	Nlagovau	For the latest in the PM's Literary Awards, follow the hashtag #PMAwards
23/07/12 10:17	Nlagovau	Julia Gillard meeting all the finalists for this year's #PMAwards http://t.co/aue8FVaU
23/07/12 10:30	Nlagovau	Julia Gillard leaving the #PMAwards http://t.co/OgAefo78
24/07/12 11:30	Nlagovau	New podcast available: http://t.co/rwqHebFt The 2012 Prime Minister's Literary Awards. #PMAwards

From this list, it is evident that in addition to the National Library of Australia's timeliness and its authority as a national literary institution, its tweets were circulated because they offered valuable extra content. Many tweets included links to interviews, podcasts or photos, including some featuring the Prime Minister, that were deemed significant by other Twitter users.

First Tuesday Book Club followed a similar approach with its tweets, announcing the winners as they happened and linking to additional content:

23/07/12 9:48	Tuesdaybookclub	Poetry winner: Luke Davies for Interferon Psalms #PMAwards
23/07/12 9:53	Tuesdaybookclub	Next up is YA fiction … And the winner is: Robert Newton for When We Were Two #PMAwards
23/07/12 9:58	Tuesdaybookclub	Children's fiction winners: Frances Watts and Judy Watson for Goodnight, Mice! #PMAwards
23/07/12 10:02	Tuesdaybookclub	Now to Non-Fiction. The winner is: Mark McKenna for An Eye for Eternity: The Life of Manning Clark #PMAwards
23/07/12 10:06	Tuesdaybookclub	Australian History is up next … And the winner is: Bill Gammage for The Biggest Estate on Earth #PMAwards
23/07/12 10:10	Tuesdaybookclub	Gillian accepting her award from the PM #PMAwards http://t.co/YBuFYibk
23/07/12 10:18	Tuesdaybookclub	All the winners on the stage! #PMawards http://t.co/xP5RF1as
23/07/12 12:54	Tuesdaybookclub	Just finished an interview with fiction winner Gillian Mears for our website. Will have all our interviews from the #PMAwards up soon!

The rapid-fire pace of these tweets – one every few minutes – coupled with the attached photographs, offer tuesdaybookclub's followers the illusion of being at the prize ceremony, a valuable asset on Twitter. The individuals who appear on the list of most mentioned tweeters, Mandy Brett and Chip Rolley, were also present at the ceremony. While these individuals lack the institutional authority of libraries or media outlets, both carry industry clout that enhances the power they derive from their eyewitness status: Rolley is a former director of the Sydney Writers' Festival and current editor of the ABC website *The Drum*, while Brett, as noted above, is an editor at Text Publishing.

The two publishers in this list of most-mentioned users both published winning titles. Allen and Unwin published winners in the fiction, non-fiction and Australian history categories, while Penguin published the winner of the young adult fiction award. These publishers were frequently mentioned by other users, despite their own more limited tweeting activity. Maintaining a presence on Twitter amplifies the capital these publishers accumulate through the prize.

Finally, the federal government again figures in this list. The prize administrator, artsculturegov, was widely retweeted. The power of this Twitter user is evident in its account statistics: despite only posting 669 tweets over the lifetime of the account to February 2013, it has 10,658 followers. The prime minister at the time of writing, Julia Gillard, appears in the list too, despite tweeting only twice. The first was a retweet from the National Library of Australia, linking to a photo of herself at the award ceremony:

23/07/12 9:56   JuliaGillard   RT @nlagovau: PM Julia Gillard speaking at the #PMAwards
http://t.co/4ANuyRgw

The second tweet offered Gillard's official Twitter statement on the awards:

23/07/12 12:07   JuliaGillard   Congratulations to the winners of the PM's Literary Awards.
Now in their 5th year, Id like to think they've become a tradition
#PMAwards JG

These comments were retweeted, and she was also mentioned by many Twitter users. For example, this tweet from Penguin Books Australia uses Gillard's name and links to a photo:

23/07/12 11:11   PenguinBooksAus   .@AnnaFunder and @JuliaGillard at the #PMawards
today. http://t.co/3Fg63Qpq

Her high profile in the Twitter conversation is an indication that the prize gave her a presence in the literary field a kind of symbolic capital that sat alongside her political authority.

The agents who tweeted the Prime Minister's Literary Awards in 2012, then, are organised by a power structure. We can further analyse the network of participants by examining the degree to which the participants interacted. Network analysis of the data set shows that the different actors were quite closely connected. The following graphic shows links between the top ten users (who are defined by counting both posts and mentions):

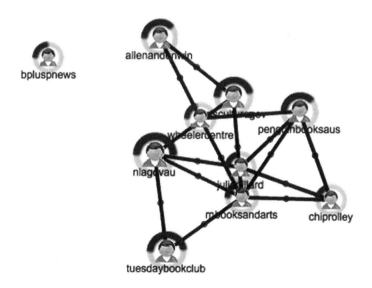

What is striking here is the very high degree of interconnection between participants. Each of these agents is connected to their own network, but most of them are also joined to each other. The same story is evident if we include all users. The figure below shows the entire field of participants, represented by diamonds. The lines between them indicate that the users are linked by a mention (the more mentions a user has, the larger the diamond symbol). Names have been removed from this diagram for increased clarity: the significance of the image is the large number of connections it shows between users.

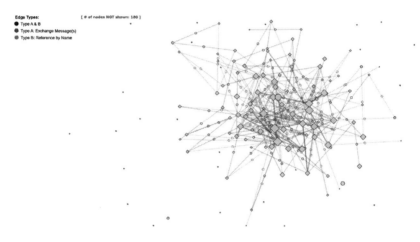

We have here a picture of an event in which people actually interacted with each other on Twitter: a real conversation, of a particular kind. The degree of connectedness suggests that Twitter can indeed be used to form relationships, a key part of developing social capital. However, as the next section shows, the window for making these connections was narrow.

When did tweeting happen: the importance of timeliness

The prize was announced on the morning of the 23 July, and this was the time when #PMAwards became a trending topic in Sydney and Melbourne. The overwhelming bulk of tweets happened in a very short period of time: 453 tweets, 73 per cent of the total, were made on the day of the announcement. There were only 13 tweets in the lead-up to the prize announcement between 17 July and 22 July, and all of these were tweets or retweets of the prize organisers, artsculturegov, or the ceremony host, nlagovau. The remainder of the tweets was made between 24 July and 6 August, indicating a gradual tailing off of interest. There were none at all after 7 August. The following figure shows posts over time (time is displayed as Eastern Standard Time, not Australian Eastern Standard Time):

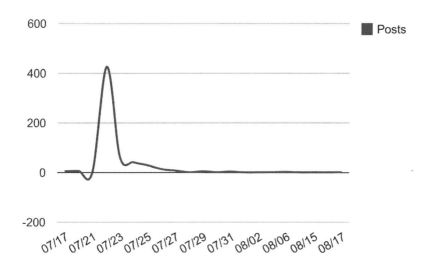

The conversation was short-lived and intense; Twitter's engagement with the Prime Minister's Award was enthusiastic but ephemeral. This data suggests that Twitter is not a place for lengthy or developed conversations, but for rapid interaction with events. Further, it highlights the brevity of the opportunity for literary organisations and people to make use of prizes to enhance their own social capital – tweeting after 24 July may have made a user appear belated, rather than timely, and consequently produced less social capital.

The Content of the Conversation: Information and Congratulations

The accumulation of social capital through this Twitter conversation was time-sensitive and organised through a tightly-connected, hierarchical network incorporating a broad cross-section of the literary field. Crucially, converting the prize into capital also required users to tweet the right sort of content.

Analysis of the collected tweets reveals a conspicuous absence of criticism and debate. The following figure shows the most commonly used words in tweets with the hashtag #PMAwards.

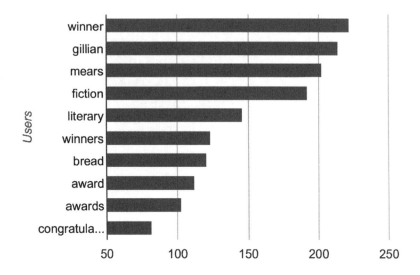

Nine of these top ten words convey bare information – 'winner' 'Gillian' 'mears' and 'fiction' for example, are the top four words, and can be combined to describe Gillian Mears as the recipient of the award for fiction. The title of her winning novel was *Foal's Bread*: 'bread' appears in the top ten words, but inconsistent apostrophe use meant that 'foal's' did not. From this list, it is evident that the award for fiction garnered the bulk of attention, rather than the awards for non-fiction, children's literature, history and poetry that were announced at the same ceremony. The concentration of interest on fiction suggests that the novel possesses more media meta-capital, and perhaps more symbolic capital, than other genres.

A high proportion of the tweets using the #PMAwards hashtag were purely informational. Such tweets include the examples from *First Tuesday Book Club* and the National Library of Australia noted above, and this tweet from Radio National's *Books and Arts Daily* program:

23/07/12 10:19   RNBooksAndArts   We'll be speaking with #PMAwards fiction winner Gillian Mears in about 20 minutes. Tune in!

Tweets such as this are miniature news bulletins, relatively neutral and absent of commentary or opinion. They perform one of the fundamental functions of Twitter, the dissemination of breaking news.

There are further layers to the work done by these informational tweets. Just by mentioning the names of the awards and the names of authors, Twitter users such as Radio National *Books and Arts Daily* and *First Tuesday Book Club* are accumulating capital. They are displaying their status as cultural insiders, building both cultural capital and symbolic capital. Further, tweets that mention names promote a connection between the Twitter user and the author, creating a tie that can develop into social capital.

The value of this work is increased by the addition of a personal tone. The only emotionally loaded word in the top ten is 'congratulations'. In fact, 'congratulations' or 'congrats' appear over 120 times: that is, in 20 per cent of the tweets. As an example, consider this tweet from The Wheeler Centre:

23/07/12 10:09   Wheelercentre   And Gillian Mears wins the Fiction Prize for Foals' Bread, her first novel in 16 years. Our hearty congrats! #PMAwards

Here, the Wheeler Centre showcases its relationship with an author – an important asset for an institution that hosts regular author events. The Wheeler Centre also adds factual detail to display its knowledge of Mears's work and increase the value of the tweet to followers.

In another example, editor Sally Heath establishes a link between herself and a winner through a congratulatory tweet:

23/07/12 10:26   heath_sally   Congratulations to Mark McKenna for winning the PM's Non Fiction Award for An Eye for Eternity. Brilliant book to work on. #PMawards

The Twitter account for the magazine *Bookseller and Publisher* offers its congratulations to a winning publisher, cementing its status as an industry-oriented publication:

23/07/12 10:50   BplusPNews   @AllenAndUnwin Congratulations for scooping three awards! #PMawards

Even when the word 'congratulations' is omitted, many of the tweets in this conversation expressed warmth. For example, critic and author James Bradley tweeted:

23/07/12 10:18   cityoftongues   Yay Gillian! So pleased. RT @ChipRolley: PM Literary Award for Fiction goes to: Gillian Mears, Foal's Bread #PMAwards

These tweets create and display a positive connection with the prizes and the authors. They establish the Twitter user as both a judge of the awards – bestowing approval on their choices – and a cultural insider who has a personal relationship with an author or publisher. The tweets are no doubt genuine expressions of pleasure and admiration, but they are also highly effective strategies for building a Twitter user's capital.

Almost all tweets fell into the two categories of informational or congratulatory. There were no tweets expressing dissatisfaction with the prizes. There are several ways in which we might interpret this lack of criticism. It is possible that across media platforms the Prime Minister's Literary Awards do not attract the vociferous critique that some other prizes do. Both the Nobel Prize and The Man Booker Prize have a history of attracting controversy, and their presence on Twitter can evoke critical responses: for example, following the announcement of Mo Yan as the winner of the 2012 Nobel Prize for Literature, Philip Roth's biographer Blake Bailey tweeted 'Mo Yan my ass. #rothscrewedagain' (Miller 2012).

A broader perspective of literary culture on social media suggests another interpretation of the positive Twitter response to the Prime Minister's Literary Awards. While much media coverage of social media highlights the spectre of the vindictive internet troll, social media can encourage self-censoring by users and a culture of niceness. Twitter's potential for immediate connection with the object of criticism can lead Twitter users to refrain from criticism in order to avoid offending authors or others. Jacob Silverman writes about this for the *Slate Book Review*: 'if you spend time in the literary Twitter- or blogospheres, you'll be positively besieged by amiability, by a relentless enthusiasm' (Silverman 2012). He is insightful on the pressure towards praise that is exerted through Twitter: 'social media's centrifugal forces of approbation – retweets, likes, favorites, and the self-consciousness that accompanies each public utterance – make any critique stick out sorely' (ibid.).

For Emmett Stinson, the prevailing online climate of literary enthusiasm is troubling because it signifies 'a consensus-culture where certain authors, who have become the literary equivalent of sacred cows, are placed beyond reproach' (2012). In the closely-connected world of Australian publishing, there may be pressure to publicly support our prize-winning authors. Certainly, the social media response to the Prime Minister's Literary Awards has been supportive. There may have been negative commentary on the Prime Minister's Literary Awards hidden elsewhere on Twitter by people who chose not to follow the hashtag protocol of the event. Analysis of the official conversation, though, reveals a process where the social capital of users is built through affirmation.

Conclusion

As a result of its increasing uptake among the publishing industry, Twitter has become a partial snapshot of the literary field: a window into its structuring relationships and activities. The case study of tweets about the 2012 Prime Minister's Literary Awards has shown a field of participants drawn from many sectors of the literary field, including government departments, libraries, broadcasters, editors, publishers, readers and booksellers. These Twitter users wrote to each other about the prize, referring to other users frequently to form an interconnected and hierarchically-structured web. To join this network and connect with influential agents, it was necessary for users to tweet rapidly – most tweets occurred in the hours immediately following the announcement of the winners.

The intense burst of activity and the high rate of participation among key literary figures make this Twitter conversation noteworthy. What may belie its significance, at least on a first reading, is the superficial content of the conversation. Yet plain informational and congratulatory tweets have profound effects. Each apparently bland tweet creates a positive connection between agents, while simultaneously displaying the cultural expertise and currency of the tweeter. Beneath the surface of a pleasant or informative tweet lies a fundamental activity of the literary field, the exchange of different forms of capital. When people or organisations associate themselves with a prize on Twitter, they mobilise and appropriate its cultural authority, media status and economic power. Twitter users may then convert these intersecting forms of capital into their own social capital – virtual links with authors, publishers, readers or even prime ministers that may over time become durable connections, a network of recognition and relationship. Although the value of these connections will vary for different institutional and personal twitter users, in each case there is the potential for social capital to contribute towards their future cultural status and economic power. Reading tweets in this way suggests that the emerging dominance of literary prizes and the spread of social media may shape the development of the 21st century literary field.

Chapter 11

THE ECONOMICS OF THE AUSTRALIAN LITERARY CLASSIC

Ivor Indyk

When I was doing my PhD in literature at London University in the 1970s, it was assumed that the literary classic was our proper object of study. Not the genesis of the work so much – this was the period in which the author ceased to be regarded as the arbiter of the work's significance, though constructions of the author might be allowed; nor the historical and social circumstances which presided over its creation, as these could only partially determine the literary classic's later significance; but its reception, the ways in which the work had been read and interpreted by successive generations of readers. For this after all is the defining feature of the literary classic – its ability to outlast its original readers, and to continue to exercise an appeal long after lesser works, even those which were immensely popular in their own period, have fallen by the wayside. The classic endures; it is enhanced not diminished by time.

In the libertarian atmosphere of the 70s, we were fond of arguing that the persistence of the classic was due to its multiplicity of meaning, to the fact that, as Frank Kermode argued in his collection of lectures titled *The Classic*, it was in the nature of the classic to be 'patient of interpretation'. This was the age of polysemy and ambiguity, plurality and undecideability, irony and aporia, qualities which the literary classic was said to have in abundance, and which ensured that no single reading, or succession of readings, could ever exhaust its potential for meaning (Kermode 1975, 75, 80, 121, 130).

I found myself in the middle of a debate, conducted across the channel, between Roland Barthes, one of the French champions of interpretative liberty and its subversive pleasures, most notably in his books *S/Z* and *The Pleasure of the Text*, and Kermode, who was my supervisor, and the voice of English moderation, in his determination to claim the liberty of interpretation for the proper workings of tradition. For Barthes the literary classic was only moderately plural: its plenitude of meanings was directed towards fruitful ends, rather like a well-stocked pantry, or a pregnant woman, to take one of his more controversial analogies. It was only in the modern work, the *texte de jouissance*, that the constraints really dropped away, and the act of interpretation, freed from subjection to any kind of authority, became so active, so generative, that the reader might in effect be thought of as the real author of the work. Hence the term Barthes used to describe this modern sort of classic – *scriptible* – as if to read it was in fact to write it (Barthes 1970; *Le plaisir du texte* 1973).

Kermode would only go part of the way down this path. 'What Barthes calls "modern",' he asserted, 'is very close to what I am calling "classic", and what he calls "classic" is very close to what I call "dead"' (Kermode, 136). That is to say, there can be no limits to the interpretive potential offered by the literary classic – it can in principle be read in many different ways, in ways as yet unknown to us – this multiplicity is what guarantees that it will outlast time. It's not clear who was being more radical – Barthes or Kermode – and yet both were restating an ancient principle in seeking to claim for the literary work, whether the classic classic or the modern classic, the capacity for an endless appeal. For the ancients this power lay in the classic's universality, *sub specie aeternitatis*, its appeal across the boundaries of place and time. For contemporary critics, in a relativistic age, it is the classic's infinite mutability, its ability to lend itself to different readings in different times, that ensures its continuity.

Those were heady days – what seems remarkable now, 40 years later, is the heroic role we readily gave to readers, and to the act of reading, in our understanding of how the literary classic worked. It is as if we imagined unbroken generations of readers, all busy in the activity of interpretation, creating their versions of the classic texts, and reinvigorating them for the generations that would follow. We never thought, for a moment, about how many readers might *actually* be involved in this process of cultural renewal and change that we so readily assumed to be taking place, still less about whether or not there would be sufficient readers to keep the books in print, so that they were available to be read in the first place. There was such pleasure to be had in reading considered as an act of writing, and such responsibility in reading considered as the subverting and remaking of convention, that one could scarcely doubt there would always be, as there always must have been, an abundance of readers to answer the call.

In fact, the idea of an abundance of active readers that we used to underwrite the idea of the literary classic's multiple readings, was in the 1970s little more than two hundred years old itself, the product of the development of a reading public from around the middle of the eighteenth century. For most of its history the classic had been sustained by a tiny readership, which was enough to ensure its passage through the generations. On the face of it, judging by the increasingly loud lamentations we hear all around us about the death and disappearance of readers, the classic is likely to revert to this condition in the future.

*   *   *

I suppose it was easy to believe that the literary classic led a vital and active life in readers' minds because in those days, when literature in English for me meant English and American literature, the classics were readily available in cheap and attractive paperback editions. The commercial considerations that underlay this availability – the fact that many of the titles were out of copyright; the division of the planet into two massive territories ruled by British and Commonwealth rights on the one hand, and the United States and the rest of the world on the other; and the economies of scale achieved by the publishers who served these large populations – well, as an academic studying in Britain, it was easy to be oblivious of these niceties, so long as one was the beneficiary of them.

It was when I started teaching and writing on Australian literature in the early 1980s, that I became aware of the disparity between the critical value attributed to the literary classic as a site of interpretation, and the haphazard existence it led in the marketplace, and in the minds of Australian readers. This was during the second part of the period we now think of as the halcyon days for Australian literature, the period between the two bicentennials in 1970 and 1988, when national self-consciousness was at its height – but even then the teaching of Australian literature was a tricky affair, requiring the reframing of courses, and the replacement of chosen texts, because the classics you wanted to impress the students with were out of print. I remember being fobbed off by publishers when I rang and told them that my course alone would sell 100 copies of their out-of-print title (which even then was an exaggeration), not understanding that they would be the only copies of the title the publisher would sell that year, and a long way short of justifying a reprint.

There are immutable facts about our vast country and its largely immigrant population which make it difficult to keep Australian classics in print, even without the supposedly devastating effects that literary theory and the destruction of the literary canon are supposed to have had on our universities. The commercial viability of Australian literary publishing – at least that part of it devoted to classic titles – is almost completely dependent on educational adoptions, since the reading public, in the course of its daily browsing, isn't likely to feed on a classic, unless some rare event, like a film adaptation, or a television mini-series, or a centenary, piques its interest. University listings might deliver sales of around 200–300 copies a year – given the tiny profit margin that attends sales on this scale, a publisher would need a large number of classics on its list, all of them being taught, to make an impact on their bottom line. The new digital printing technologies make it possible to do print runs of 500 copies, or even 200 copies, at a reasonable rate, which means that you can't lose money on a small reprint – but you can't make money either.

It is different for high school adoptions, but only if the book is set for the 'general' courses – the higher the level at which the book is studied for the HSC or the GCE, the lower the number of students. When Giramondo had Judith Beveridge's *Wolf Notes* set for the most advanced English course on the Victorian GCE, it would sell 500 copies a year and dropping – because once there were copies in the system, they were available to be read by the following year's students as well. So unless the title is set for a general course, where sales might be at a very respectable 3000–5000 copies a year, and more, the value of a high school adoption will not be much greater than that of a university adoption. Of course, only a few are chosen for widespread study, and for particular educational reasons, suited to the criteria proposed by the high school English syllabus, and the likely interests of young adult readers. Of all David Malouf's books, it is one of his lesser known works, *Fly Away Peter*, that has been the most favoured by high school teachers – it is short, it is about the First World War, and it is strong on landscape. In poetry Judith Wright and Les Murray dominate the field. Tim Winton's *Cloudstreet* is an all-time favourite, its sales now in excess of 1,000,000 copies. The continued setting of David Williamson's two plays *The Club* and *The Removalists* over decades has subsidised Currency Press's wide-ranging publication of contemporary Australian drama.

It is important, clearly, that the chosen title should be aligned with a landmark event or epoch in Australian history, or raise issues about place and society that can be discussed in the classroom. In this respect, the economy of the classics backlist is not all that different from that of the commercially-oriented frontlist – it depends largely on topicality, or an appeal to broad

Australian themes, or issues of social relevance. Books which display a pronounced literary quality, which push the boundaries of form, or contest the attributes of a genre, may at best find their way onto a small university course. Otherwise, most of Australia's literary classics will be in a kind of waking sleep for most of the time, selling enough to keep themselves alive, which is to say, to render themselves eligible for the subsidy provided in the total economy of the publisher by other more popular and better-selling titles.

I had a conversation recently with Michael Heyward, about Text's new classics series, in which I expressed my admiration for the amount of thought, and planning, and money, that had gone into the series. Heyward replied with words to the effect of, 'You can't be an Australian literary publisher, and not have a backlist of classics'. I understood him to mean that, as a commercial publisher, there might be much in Text's frontlist that wasn't necessarily literary, but the publishing house would be judged finally by the quality of its backlist. I felt like saying, 'I think of Giramondo as a literary publisher, because its frontlist titles are classics.' I couldn't say this aloud, because it would have sounded foolhardy, and it wouldn't have made any sense. Since it is in the nature of a classic to persist in time, indeed to prove itself in time, how can you know that a recently published book is a classic? And since, even if the book should turn out to be a classic, it will take a long time for this to be recognised, how can you hope to sell substantial copies on this basis now?

I blame this foolhardy attitude on the fact that I was originally trained as a critic on books that had had plenty of time to become classics before they became the regular subject of scholarly criticism. Then I was living in the literary past, in blissful ignorance of commercial realities; now I am living in the future, and find myself equally at odds with those realities. When considering the economics of the classic, it is important to distinguish between the publication of books that are already widely regarded as classics, but have fallen out of copyright or out of print – and the publication of books which you think will be classics but which must somehow make their way in the marketplace in the meantime. In the former case, supported by a commercial frontlist, the classics backlist may be a risky undertaking, but it should be able to pay for itself, and it brings in addition the benefit of literary prestige – an important asset for a literary publisher, but one that is impossible to measure in commercial terms. For a publisher to have a frontlist of classics, or rather of books that it hopes will be classics in the future, is to be the recipient of even greater prestige, but it leaves open the question of where the money to run the business will come from, if the books are not going to sell in large quantities now.

The answer to this question is, unashamedly, patronage. It has long been known that patronage is an essential ingredient in the literary economy, the only thing that will bridge the distance opened up by the classic between the present fact of publication, and the delayed act of recognition. Perhaps this hasn't been understood enough in Australia, where patronage seeks immediate satisfaction, preferably in physical or visual terms, hence the money that goes to support concerts, opera and the like.

In the case of Giramondo, for every dollar earnt in sales, the equivalent of two dollars is received in patronage, primarily in kind from the University of Western Sydney, which provides support through salaries, accommodation and equipment, and to a smaller extent in cash, through a publishing subsidy from the Literature Board of the Australia Council, which defrays the cost of around seven literary titles a year. This support allows Giramondo to operate with the commercial aim, not of making of a profit, but of covering its production costs, an ambition which leaves a lot of room for literary idealism, and for a belief in providence.

There are also other, less obvious forms of patronage. Perhaps the most powerful of these is the system of high school adoptions I referred to earlier. When an author is set for a general course – as is the case with Tim Winton and Kate Grenville, David Malouf and Les Murray, David Williamson and Louis Nowra – the ensuing sales can be so large, that they serve to subsidise the more innovative and less popular literary titles of the publishing house concerned. This is the case with Winton at Penguin and Williamson at Currency Press. It's odd to think of high school students as the biggest patrons of Australian literature, the ones who ensure that it will continue to be published, but as a group, they are the single largest contributor to our literary economy.

* * *

I would like to return to the question which I left lurking in my account of how the literary classic appeared to us in the 1970s, as an inexhaustible text constantly renewed in the present by the interpretive agility of its readers. How should we view the literary classic now, when one of its defining characteristics appears to be that it has no readers, or few? It is one of the easiest gestures for a critic to make these days, to extol the virtues of an Australian classic, and then to exclaim, with an air of astonishment, that it is out of print. Of course it is out of print, that is what makes it an Australian literary classic! Nor is this necessarily a bad thing. Years of printing Australian classics when the times were good, by such publishers as Angus & Robertson, Penguin, Rigby and Heinemann, means that there is a substantial second-hand supply of texts for those who need it. In the early 1980s, when I was doing the bulk of my reading in Australian literature, most of the books were out of print, and I read them in editions which were then at least twenty years old, bought from remainder tables in second-hand bookstores.

In any case, these days the presence of ebooks mean that all our classics can be made available without being in print; and digital technology ensures that they can be brought into print in small numbers if the need arises. It is not as if they are in immediate danger of disappearing. Critics will return to them, and give them a new and relevant reading one day. They may do well to think of the publication of their criticism in a scholarly journal as akin to their rolling up their reading and putting it in a tree, since if there are few readers for our classics, there are even less readers for the readers of our classics. Perhaps the best way to think of our classics is as *churingas*, and the libraries and the backlists which house them as the modern equivalent of caves. For those who visit, and take them up, they will exercise their magic; but for most Australians, it will be enough simply to know that they are there. The distinction doesn't really affect the power of the classic, which will exercise its magic, regardless of how many people take it up and read it, or when in the future they will do so.

Chapter 12

MAKING THE LIST

The Value of Prizes for Women Writers in the Construction of
Educational Reading Lists

Sophie Allan and Beth Driscoll

'Every girl who writes needs a bucket of cash to be thrown over her at
least once in her life, so she can soldier on, and even feel for a while that
it's been worth the torture.'

– Helen Garner

In April 2013, the $50,000 Stella Prize for Australian women's writing was
awarded for the first time. Speaking at the event, Helen Garner showed an
acute awareness of female writers' particular need for both economic support
and encouragement. This need springs from systemic gender biases that
operate in contemporary literary culture. The annual surveys undertaken by
VIDA: Women in Literary Arts show a consistent predominance of men as
both reviewers and reviewees in some of the United States' most respected
publications (VIDA 2013). These statistics are echoed in Australia by the
findings of Rebecca Starford, who surveyed several Australian publications
(Case 2011). In 2009 and 2011, the shortlists for Australia's most prestigious
literary award, the Miles Franklin, were composed entirely of books written
by men, raising the visibility of the considerable gender imbalance that exists
in the world of literature and publishing.

This gender disparity is also present in the education system. Louise
Swinn, one of the founders of the Stella Prize and co-director of independent
press, Sleepers Publishing, has spoken of the boon of having the first novel
she published win *The Age* Book of the Year Award in 2009 (Swinn 2013).
Things We Didn't See Coming, by Steven Amsterdam, was subsequently

added to the text list for the Victorian Certificate for Education (VCE) Year 12 English subject, where it remained for three years. The VCE plays a pivotal role in the Victorian education system as the dominant pathway to tertiary education, and its syllabus offers powerful endorsement to particular texts. The movement from publication by a small independent press, to formal recognition in the form of a literary prize, to consecration by the education system, is a flow of documentable events that illuminates the somewhat mystical nature of the bestowal of literary merit. The gender of the author is a factor in this process. At an International Women's Day panel discussion at Readings bookstore in 2011, Swinn held up a brochure for seminars about fifteen VCE texts, thirteen of which were written by men, and stated, 'These are kids going through school and this is what they're reading. And then we tell the girls that their voices are just as worthwhile' (Case 2011). The inequity that exists in the literary world and in the education system sends a message to young women that their voices are not, in fact, worthwhile.

The Stella Prize was designed to address this field-wide discrimination against women's writing. Its name is a direct response to the Miles Franklin Literary Award, founded through a stipulation set out in the will of Australian author Stella Maria Sarah 'Miles' Franklin. When Franklin's *My Brilliant Career* was published in 1901 it was published under a man's name, a practice that continues today. Carrie Tiffany, the inaugural winner of the Stella Prize, notes that the prize restores Franklin's true name and therefore her gender (ABC Radio 2013). To assess the prize's potential impact, this paper examines the VCE text lists for English from the last ten years and the projected list for 2014, and analyses the data to assess the relationship between gender, prizes and consecration by the education system. These results are discussed in the context of gender in contemporary literary culture and Bourdieu's theories of literary production, particularly his 'circuits of legitimation': 'systems of sponsorship, evaluation, and consecration by means of which power euphemizes itself as merit (as intrinsic and proper rather than imposed and arbitrary) and thereby secures its symbolic efficacy' (Bourdieu 1990 66–67). A prize exclusively for women, such as the Stella, ensures that a female-authored book will enter the public discourse every year as a prize winner. If there is a direct link in the VCE data between prize winners and books studied in high schools in Victoria, this will go some way to prove the comment of Stella Prize founding patron Ellen Koshland, that the Stella Prize is a 'landscape changer' for Australian literature (Koshland 2013).

Gender in Contemporary Literary Culture

The arena of serious reading and writing has largely excluded women, as well as other non-dominant groups of society. In Australia, the literary tradition entrenches particular national ideologies that exclude women. In a recent article published in *Meanjin* following the emergence of the Stella Prize, Julieanne Lamond writes, 'There have been concerns that the [Miles Franklin] prize perpetuates the idea that certain kinds of experiences (blokes, the past, the bush) are more representatively Australian than others' (2013, 33). The idea that certain experiences are accepted as representative of Australia in literature is problematic for those who fall outside of these stereotypes, among them, women. What Lamond commented on in 2013 was apparent to Giulia Giuffre nearly 30 years ago. Her essay, *To be Australian, a Woman, and a Writer*, notes that 'while the large, received (or debated) Australian legends and myths may or may not be true of individual men, they are clearly inadequate in any discussion of women because they simply do not even acknowledge their existence' (1987, 4). The omission of women is not confined to the stories we consecrate into the Australian literary canon, but also extends to their exclusion from the construction of serious reading and writing practices (Driscoll 2008b). Martyn Lyons suggests that the practices of 'serious' reading and writing were deemed 'inappropriate for women, since they lacked the cerebral capacity for sustained reasoning' (2001, 373). Women have been cast historically as readers of fiction, romance and magazines, and their reading patterns, largely carved out at the mercy of their household duties have been described as intermittent and 'interstitial' (Lyons 2001, 374). As Lyons states, this is an ideology that is perpetuated in the publishing industry through contemporary female-directed marketing campaigns for cookbooks, women's magazines and romance novelettes (2001, 371).

Women writers have been treated as dismissively as women readers. The perceived subject matter of women's writing has been one reason it has been largely omitted from the modern literary canon, lists of prize winners, and thus educational reading lists: the writing of women has been said to be less concerned with 'important' themes such as war (Goldsworthy 2013), and often set in the home or to do with family, which has seen it dismissed as 'trivial, domestic, narrow' (Giuffre 1987, 9). However, Jonathan Franzen's *Freedom* was incorporated into a list created by men's magazine *GQ*, 'The new canon: The 21 books from the 21st century every man should read' because Franzen 'wrote the two best books [of the millennium] on, among other things, family, anti-anxiety, drugs, marriage…' (*GQ*, 2013). In this case, when a man writes about the domestic it is seen as far from trivial.

The treatment of women writers is summed up effectively by Giuffre, 'The only reason why one has to specify "woman" writer is that a writer is assumed male until proven otherwise' (1987, 5). This point, made in 1987, holds true globally today. An article in *The Atlantic*, '21 books written by and about women that men would benefit from reading' (2013), lamented that the *GQ* 'new canon' had contained only three books written by women, but in fact the list actually included books by four women, one of whom, Jhumpa Lahiri, it can be assumed was incorrectly understood to be a man, as she does not have an instantly recognisably Western female name. This situation reinforces twofold the invisibility of female writers in Western literary culture, and shows just how entrenched this invisibility is. The *GQ* article cordons off the arena of male reading and writing as a place for men and men's themes almost exclusively, and the *Atlantic* article, while making a valuable point, fails to see a woman writer where she exists, assuming her to be male – the cultural norm for a writer.

Using Bourdieu to Theorise Gender, Prizes and the Education System

Bourdieu's model of the literary field offers a useful mechanism for tracking the circulation of texts, authors and institutions in literary culture. However, his work is noticeably silent on the issue of gender (Adkins 2004, 2). *The Rules of Art* (1996) and *The Field of Cultural Production* (1993) do not specifically engage with gender issues, and his one publication on the subject, *Masculine Domination* (2001), deals only in general terms with gender and is primarily based on research material from 1950s Algeria. Bourdieu's model neglects any discussion of the interaction of gender politics with the activity of specific literary fields. As Bridget Fowler notes, 'Bourdieu's work was largely restricted to analyzing the *structural constants* of masculine domination. He never sufficiently elaborated on the different types of patriarchy and their connection *historically* with different fields of power' (2003, 479). However, despite Bourdieu's minimal treatment of gender, his model can be stretched to allow for productive analyses of women's experiences in literary culture, as outlined by Toril Moi in 'Appropriating Bourdieu: Feminist Theory and Pierre Bourdieu's Sociology of Culture' (1991) and applied in Beth Driscoll's analysis of Oprah's Book Club (2008b).

A 2008 study by Marysa Demoor et al. focused, as this paper does, on the relationship between the literary prize and gender, employing the theories of Bourdieu in their discussion. Across four genres (prose, poetry, plays, children's literature), the study found that men overwhelmingly dominated the roles of judge, entrant and winner of prizes in Flanders and the Netherlands, except in the genre of children's fiction. This was the only genre with close to equal gender representation (Demoor et al. 2008, 37). Demoor and her co-authors draw on Bourdieu's definitions of different types of capital to explain the significance of their findings, suggesting that the genres of drama and poetry are associated with a very high level of symbolic capital in Flanders and 'perhaps not unpredictably, are male-encoded', with almost no women winning prizes in these categories (2008, 29). The way prizes are enmeshed in different forms of capital is discussed in Beth Driscoll's paper in the present volume, and is equally relevant in a discussion of gender, prizes and curriculum.

One of the most useful Bourdieusian tools for an investigation of gender and literary prizes is his concept of 'symbolic violence', which denotes the subordination of the art of a non-dominant group (1993, 121; 137). Systems that perform a consecratory function are in a position to exert this violence: and two of the most important such systems are literary prizes and educational institutions. A 'circuit of legitimation' links these two institutions; prizes bestow literary merit, and education systems go on to create consumers with aligned value systems.

The contemporary literary prize is a complex phenomenon sustained by media visibility. James English suggests that literary prizes are able to flourish in any situation where they are being paid attention: even if they are criticised for making wrong decisions, the notion of aesthetic value that they are based upon is acknowledged (2002, 115–116). Amongst those who champion prizes, the collective belief in their value continues to inflate, springboarding into cross-media marketing campaigns, literary festival appearances, reviews, book club selection, radio and television appearances and so on (Driscoll 2008a, 176). The result is that literary prizes increasingly set the terms for which books are 'in the air'. As

Australian critic Geordie Williamson writes, 'The whole machinery of publishing and bookselling now organises itself around the most visible awards' (2010).

Media discussions of prizes may assume that pure aesthetic value exists, completely separated from social factors such as gender. However, as Bourdieu has said, the elevation of one set of values as more sacred than another is symbolic violence (Bourdieu 1993, 121; 137). This 'violence' begins very early in the education of young people. Like prize culture, the education system is a 'system specifically designed to fulfill a consecration function' (ibid.). Schools legitimise specific literary texts by cultivating familiarity and appreciation of them (ibid., 121). Schools also endorse particular reading practices and foster students' disposition towards the 'pursuit of culture' (ibid., 233). This dual process, consecrating works and shaping readers, draws the line between legitimate and illegitimate forms of culture and ways of dealing with culture. There is thus a nexus between the teaching of reading within the education system and ideas about the value of books in our society.

Gender, Prizes and VCE Text Lists 2004–2014

In order to consider the relationship between gender, prize-winning and addition to the curriculum, this paper analyses VCE reading lists from 2004–2014. Each of these includes between eleven and fourteen works of literature. Year twelve English teachers select a subset of these books for their students to study and write on in their end-of-year exams. A text list is a form of canon, and is susceptible to various kinds of scrutiny: for the inclusion of women, of writers from different cultural backgrounds and more. In order to gain a sense of the process of selection for these texts, an interview was undertaken with Greg Houghton, an English educator who sat on the selection panel for several years in the early 2000s.

Official guidelines (VCAL 2013) state that each text selected for the VCE English text lists will:

- have literary merit and be worthy of close study
- be an excellent example of form and genre
- sustain intensive study, raising interesting issues and providing challenging ideas
- be appropriate for both male and female students

- be appropriate for the age and development of students and, in that context, reflect current community standards and expectations.

The text list as a whole will:

- be suitable for a wide range of students, including second language students
- reflect the cultural diversity of the Victorian community
- include a balance of new and established works
- include texts that display affirming perspectives (VCAL 2013).

Houghton emphasises that these guidelines were adhered to strenuously (Houghton 2013). However, of interest was how the books actually come to be nominated for selection. Each year there are only a handful of new books to select, as the text list is a rotational one, with most books getting four years on the list. Houghton says that the books that get suggested for consideration by the panel are ones that members believe fit within the official guidelines; that they have a strong personal response to; and that they regard as most likely to work well in the Year 12 English classroom. The members of the panel apply to sit on the panel, and are selected based on their professional experience as English educators. Women are well represented on the panel, as is to be expected, given their numbers in Secondary English teaching more generally (ibid.). Houghton did not, however, recall the panel making any deliberate attempt to achieve some kind of overall gender balance on the VCE text list. It was more a matter of, as above, working within the guidelines to find books that students could readily and meaningfully engage with.

In response to a question about the influence of prizes on nominations, Houghton acknowledged that, yes, the group was made up of the sort of people who are fairly familiar with the literary scene and with prize winners, and although this may not be a conscious factor in the decision, the name of the author and book is 'in the air' (ibid.). This attests to the success of prizes in marketing books, and their efficacy in bestowing literary merit.

The first step in analysing the data was to identify the gender of each author. Table 1 shows the percentage of books on the text list written by women. Female-authored books made up between 18 per cent and 42 per cent of each of the English text lists. The average over the 11 years was 32 per cent, or a little less than a third.

Year	Percentage of books written by female authors
2004	38
2005	38
2006	29
2007	18
2008	25
2009	25
2010	42
2011	33
2012	33
2013	38
2014	33
Average	32

Table 1. Gender representation on VCE English Lists
2004 – 2014

These results show consistent under-representation of women authors in the text lists for the VCE English subject. Such inequality has significant effects on literary culture, as students are taught to understand the literary canon as consisting mostly of work written by men. Britta Zangen, writing about the Orange Prize (now Bailey's Prize), states that the male-dominated canon encourages the idea that men are better writers than women: 'Without anyone rubbing this in, or even commenting on it at all, the message is self-evident, the fact so obvious, that girls eventually end up valuing men's writings more than women's by the time they are adults' (2003, 289–290). As a consequence, it may also be less common for female students to conceive of themselves as writers than their male counterparts. The literature provided for children and young adults supplies the 'images, the story lines, and the language to use in constructing ourselves as people who belong on one side of the gender divide or the other' (Cherland 2008, 279).

The next step in our study involved analysing the lists to identify which books had won prizes, and which prizes they had won. This information was gathered from authors' personal websites, publishers' websites, and prizes' websites. However, due to the proliferation of prizes in contemporary literary culture there is the possibility that less publicised, more obscure prizes have been overlooked.

As part of this analysis, a subcategory was created for books published post-1957. We chose this date because the number and profile of prizes increased dramatically in the second half of the twentieth century. Most of the literary prizes that attract attention today were created during this time: for example, the Miles Franklin Literary Award in 1957, the Man Booker Prize in 1968, the Whitbread Book of the Year (now Costa Book of the Year) in 1971, and the Victorian Premier's Literary Awards in 1985. This paper takes 1957 as the cut off for its analysis as reflecting the importance of the second half of the twentieth century and as a meaningful date for Australian literary culture with the founding of the Miles Franklin Literary Award, Australia's first national literary prize. We expected our data to reflect the increasing dominance of the prize as a means of determining literary credibility for books published in the second half of the twentieth and beginning of the twenty-first centuries.

Table 2 shows that the percentage of books on the lists that won awards ranged from 29 per cent to 69 per cent, with an average of 48 per cent. For books published after 1957, these numbers are significantly higher: between 44 per cent and 100 per cent of books on the list published after 1957 have won awards, with an average of 71 per cent.

Year	Books on the list that won prizes (as a percentage)	Books on the list, published after 1957, that won prizes (as a percentage).
2004	38	50
2005	31	44
2006	29	50
2007	36	57
2008	42	63
2009	42	63
2010	42	63
2011	67	89
2012	67	100
2013	69	100
2014	67	100
Average	48	71

Table 2. Prize-winning books on VCE English Lists 2004 – 2014

One of the most striking aspects of this analysis is the jump that occurs in 2011. From 2013 onwards, 100 per cent of books on the list published after

1957 had won prizes. This may indicate that the importance of prizes has grown substantially in the past few years.

The lists were then separated into books written by men and women, and analysis was done on how many books in those categories had won prizes. The percentage of female-authored books on the list that won prizes ranged from 20 per cent to 80 per cent with an average of 54 per cent. When male-authored texts were isolated, the figures were slightly lower, with between 14 and 75 per cent of listings having won prizes (on average 46 per cent). For both categories, there is a trend where books on the list are increasingly likely to be prize winners.

Year	How many of the books by women on the list had won a prize?	As a percentage	How many of the books by men on the list had won a prize?	As a percentage
2004	1/5	20	4/8	50
2005	1/5	20	3/8	38
2006	1/4	25	3/10	30
2007	1/2	50	3/9	33
2008	2/3	67	3/9	33
2009	2/3	67	3/9	33
2010	4/5	80	1/7	14
2011	3/4	75	5/8	63
2012	3/4	75	5/8	63
2013	3/5	60	6/8	75
2014	2/4	50	6/8	75
Average		54		46

Table 3. Prize-winning Male- and Female-authored books

Overall, books on the text list by women are more likely to have won prizes than books on the list by men, indicating that prizes may be more important for female authors in gaining a place on the education curriculum.

As seen in Table 2, books published after 1957 that appear on the VCE lists are more likely to have won a prize: 71 per cent of recently-published books on the list have won prizes, compared to 48 per cent of all books. The subcategory of recently-published books can be broken down by gender:

Year	How many of the books by women on the list, published after 1957, had won a prize?	As a percentage	How many of the books by men on the list, published after 1957, had won a prize?	As a percentage
2004	1/4	25	4/6	67
2005	1/4	25	3/5	60
2006	1/3	33	3/7	43
2007	1/2	50	3/5	60
2008	2/3	67	3/5	60
2009	2/3	67	3/5	60
2010	4/5	80	1/3	33
2011	3/3	100	5/5	100
2012	3/3	100	5/5	100
2013	3/3	100	6/6	100
2014	2/2	100	6/6	100
Average		68		71

Table 4. Prize-winning Male- and Female-Authored Books Published after 1957

On an initial reading, these figures suggest that prizes may be slightly more important for men than women in the case of recently published books. However, this slight difference is eclipsed by the fact that since 2011, all of the post-1957 books on the list, by both men and women, have won prizes.

There is a very clear relationship between prize-winning and selection for the VCE English lists. This relationship becomes significantly stronger for books published after 1957: books that perhaps aren't yet 'classics' and need to prove their place in this canon in some other way. A female-authored book is 9 per cent more likely to have won a prize than its male-authored counterpart on the whole, and after 1957, a male-authored book is 3 per cent more likely to have won a prize. However, the absolute figures show the consistent domination of the lists by books by men, reinforcing the idea that women need prizes as a way of increasing their representation.

In Bourdieusian terms, these results show that the symbolic capital associated with a prize can exert significant effects in the forming of literary canons such as school text lists. There is a powerful circuit of legitimation at work in literary culture, whereby the legitimation bestowed by a literary prize can directly translates into further consecration by the education system. While not all prize-winning books end up on the school syllabus, since 2011, surprisingly, there have been no recently published books on the VCE text list that have not won a prize.

Bourdieu's concept of 'symbolic violence' is clearly at work here, too. The notion that text lists are decided on factors such as merit or 'teachability' belies the situation of symbolic violence at work in contemporary literary culture. Books by women are much less likely to appear on the VCE text list at all, and are slightly more likely to have won prizes than books by men, indicating the prizes may have an important role to play in redressing discrimination against women in the literary field.

The Different Prizes Represented on the VCE Text Lists

Finally, our study looked at which prizes were won by the books on the VCE text lists. These were varied (see Appendix 1). Among the Australian awards won by books on the lists are the Miles Franklin Award, which appears twice, and *The Age* Book of the Year Award, which appears three times. International prizes awarded to books on the list include the Whitbread/ Costa Book of the Year, which appears three times and the John D. Criticos Prize for Greek Literature, which appears once. There are prominent, prestigious prizes on the list, but less affluent and more narrowly defined prizes also appear (the David Unaipon Award for unpublished Indigenous writers, $5000 plus publication of manuscript by University of Queensland Press). Notably absent from the VCE lists is a winner of the Orange Prize for Fiction, now known as the Baileys Women's Prize for Fiction, launched in the United Kingdom in 1996 under very similar circumstances to the Stella Prize in Australia. There are two Nobel Prize-winning authors on the VCE English lists (Ernest Hemingway and Albert Camus), but their titles have not been counted in this study, as the prize is awarded for an author's career-long contribution.

While many prizes appear on the lists, it is important to bear in mind that all prizes are not created equal. Many factors can affect the potency of a prize as a consecrator of literature, including its sponsors, judges and previous winners, its scope, its cash value and its ability to secure media attention (see English 2002, 113). Although a hierarchy exerts itself within the field of prizes, the variety of prizes apparent on the VCE lists is evidence that even a small prize is capable of elevating 'the one above the many', as Tiffany put it in her Stella Award acceptance speech (ABC Radio 2013). On being awarded the $50,000 Stella Prize, Tiffany offered $10,000 to be divided between the prize's shortlist, stating that this award 'could be a way of celebrating the many rather than the one' (ABC Radio 2013). This gesture, at odds with the traditional form and function of a literary prize, reveals the ability of the prize to empower members of non-dominant groups of society to enact their own philosophies in the field of cultural production.

Conclusion

Can the Stella Prize make a different to gender inequity in literary culture? Some commentators have questioned whether the Stella Prize further 'ghetto-ises' women's writing, and whether it is needed at all – despite the statistical evidence of gender imbalance – in an industry where women form the majority of the workers (ABC Radio, 2011). The first Miles Franklin longlist released following the emergence of the Stella was made up of eight women out of ten, as though to prove a women-only prize redundant. However, this occurrence has been described as nothing more than a 'blip' on the radar by Stella co-founder and editor at Affirm Press, Aviva Tuffield (Evans 2013). At this stage, with the historical trend as the only available framework through which to view the Miles Franklin longlist, it is impossible not to agree with Tuffield's comment (women have only won the 56-year-old prize 15 times). What the present study has shown is that winning prizes is an important route to consecration in contemporary literary culture.

This paper has examined relationships between gender, prize-winning and consecration in the education system through its analysis of data taken from the VCE English text lists from 2004–2014. The data was used to determine how women were represented in the lists, how prize winners were represented in the lists, and how these factors were related. Women were represented poorly; on average only making up 32 per cent of a VCE list. It was found that, on the whole, 54 per cent of female-authored books had won literary prizes, as opposed to 46 per cent of male-authored books. For books published after 1957, these figures grew, and the gender gap closed up, with 68 per cent of female-authored books, and 71 per cent of male-authored books having won prizes. This suggests that for both male and female authors a prize is something like a 'golden ticket' in gaining recognition by the education system. Either that, or it is a hurdle requirement, particularly since 2011. This was somewhat reinforced by the testimony of Greg Houghton, who admitted that the names of prize winners were 'in the air' when selectors were considering books to nominate for the VCE lists (2013).

These results have significance as part of a broader debate about women's place in literary culture as readers and writers. Bourdieu's theories of symbolic violence and circuits of legitimation shed light on the ways that prize culture and the education system act as consecrators of literary merit. The education system has a role in shaping consumers with socially constructed aesthetics, who will go on to teach these values in turn. The literature used as the tools of education has a major role in the communication of these values, which have historically treated women as less capable readers and writers than men.

The data from the VCE English lists confirms the idea that the literary landscape, prize culture and the education system is imbalanced in favour of men. Literary culture perpetuates white, male values, which are continually consecrated and communicated through education. The question, then, is whether the creation of a literary prize for women could have the potential to debunk some of the ingrained cultural values that persist in the modern Western world. The data would suggest that, yes, the annual production of a female prizewinner, who can enter into the circuit of festivals, be reviewed and discussed, and benefit from the discussion around literary merit provoked by prizes, could contribute to more female-authored books being adopted into the syllabus. With this, the voices, values and characters of women would have something closer to an equal footing in the cultural education of the young adults who will go on to bestow literary merit themselves.

APPENDIX 1

Book

	Author	Year Published	Prize?	Name of Award	Year of Award
A Christmas Carol	Charles Dickens	1843	NO		
A Farewell to Arms	Ernest Hemingway	1929	NO		
A Lesson Before Dying	Ernest J. Gaines	1993	YES	National Book Critics Circle Award	1993
Blueprints for a Barbed-Wire Canoe	Wayne Macauley	2004	NO		
Border Crossing	Pat Barker	2001	NO		
Brooklyn	Colm Toibin	2009	YES	Costa Novel of the Year	2009
Cat's Eye	Margaret Atwood	1988	YES	Toronto Book of the Year	1989
				Torgi Talking Book	1989
				Coles Book of the Year	1989
Cloud Street	Tim Winton	1991	YES	Miles Franklin Award	1992
Enduring Love	Ian McEwan	1997	NO		
Fly Away Peter	David Malouf	1982	YES	*The Age* Book of the Year Award	1982
				Australian Literature Society Gold Medal	1983
Generals Die in Bed	Charles Yale Harrison	1930	NO		
Hard Times	Charles Dickens	1854	NO		
Home	Larissa Behrendt	2002	YES	David Unaipon Award	2002
				Commonwealth Writers' Prize: Best First Book, South East Asia and South Pacific	2005
I for Isobel	Amy Witting	1990	NO		

I'm Not Scared	Ammaniti Niccolo	2001	NO		
In the Country of Men	Hisham Matar	2006	YES	Royal Society of Literature Ondaatje Prize	2007
In the Lake of the Woods	Tim O'Brien	1995	YES	James Fenimore Cooper Prize for Best Historical Fiction	1995
Life of Pi	Yann Martel	2001	YES	Man Booker Prize	2002
				Boeke Prize	2003
Maestro	Peter Goldsworthy	1989			
Night Street	Kristel Thornell	2010	YES	Australian/Vogel Literary Award	2009
				Dobbie Literary Award	2011
				Barbara Ramsden Award	2010
				Andrew Eiseman Award	2011
Nineteen Eighty-Four	George Orwell	1949	NO		
No Great Mischief	Alistair McLeod	1999	YES	Trillium Book Award	1999
				Thomas Head Raddall Award	2000
				International IMPAC Dublin Literary Award	2001
Of Love and Shadows	Isabelle Allende	1985	NO		
Ransom	David Malouf	2009	YES	John D. Criticos Prize for Greek Literature	2009
Spies	Michael Frayn	2002	YES	Whitbread Book of the Year	2002
Tess of the D'Urbervilles	Thomas Hardy	1891	NO		
The Accidental Tourist	Anne Tyler	1985	YES	National Book Critics Circle Award	1985
The Catcher in the Rye	J.D. Salinger	1951	NO		
The Chant of Jimmie Blacksmith	Thomas Kenneally	1972	NO		

The Curious Incident of the Dog in the Nighttime	Mark Haddon	2003	YES	Whitbread Book of the Year	2003
				Commonwealth Writers' Prize: Best First Book	2004
				Guardian Children's Fiction Prize	2003
				Boeke Prize	2003
The Girl with the Pearl Earring	Tracy Chevalier	1999	NO		
The Hunter	Julia Leigh	1999	YES	Betty Trask Award	2000
				Prix d'Astrolabe	2001
				New York Times Notable Book of the Year	2001
The Kite Runner	Khaled Hosseini	2003	YES	Boeke Prize	2004
The Member of the Wedding	Carson McCullers	1946	NO		
The Plague	Albert Camus	1947	NO		
The Quiet American	Graham Greene	1955	NO		
The Reluctant Fundamentalist	Mohsin Hamid	2007	YES	New York Times Notable Book of the Year	2007
				Ambassador Book Award of the English Speaking Union	2008
				Anisfield-Wolf Book Award	2008
				Asian American Literary Award	2008
				South Bank Show Annual Award for Literature	2008
				Premio Speciale Dal Testo Allo Schermo	2009
The Secret River	Kate Grenville	2005	YES	The Commonwealth Writers' Prize	2006

				New South Wales Premier's Literary Awards: Community Relations Commission Award	2006
				The Australian Booksellers' Award	2006
				The Australian Book Industry Prize for Book of the Year	2006
				The Australian Book Industry Prize for Literary Fiction	2006
				The Fellowship of Australian Writers' Prize for Fiction	2006
The Wife of Martin Guerre	Janet Lewis	1941	NO		
The Year of Living Dangerously	Christopher Koch	1978	YES	National Book Council Award for Australian Literature	1979
				The Age Book of the Year Award	1978
Things Fall Apart	Chinua Achebe	1958	NO		
Things We Didn't See Coming	Steven Amsterdam	2009	YES	*The Age* Book of the Year Award	2009
Tirra Lirra by the River	Jessica Anderson	1978	YES	Miles Franklin Award	1978
Triage	Scott Anderson	1998	NO		
Wuthering Heights	Emily Bronte	1847	NO		
Year of Wonders	Geraldine Brooks	2001	YES	New York Times Notable Book of the Year	2001
				Washington Post Notable Book of the Year	2001

WORKS CITED

ABC Radio. 2013. *Weekend Arts: The Culture of Prize Giving*. 13 April.
———. 2013. 'Carrie Tiffany's Stella Prize Speech'. Accessed on 8 July 2013 from www.abc.net.au/radionational/programs/booksandartsdaily/4634620.
———. 2011. *The Book Show: New Study Finds Gender Inequality in Kids' Books*. 24 May.
———. 2011. *The Book Show: Does Australia Need a Writer's Prize for Women?* 24 May.
Abrams, Dennis. 2013. 'E-book Sales are Flattening Out: Are Tablets to Blame?' 9 August. www.publishingperspectives.com.
Adkins, Lisa. 2004. 'Introduction: Feminism, Bourdieu and After'. *The Sociological Review*. 52:s2: 1–18.
The Age. 'Australian Publishers Be Damned'. 2012. 20 January. Accessed on 23 May 2013 from www.smh.com.au/opinion/society-and-culture/australian-publishers-be-damned-20120119-1q8en.html.
Allday, Alen. 2013. 'Newspaper Publishing in Australia'. IBISWorld Industry Report J5411. July.
Allen, Matthew. 2012. 'Gaining a Past, Losing a Future: Web 2.0 and Internet Historicity'. *Media International Australia*. May 143: 99–109.
Alvord, S. H. 2004. 'Social Entrepreneurship and Societal Transformation: An Exploratory Study'. *Journal of Applied Behavioral Science*. 40:3: 260–82.
Anderson, Benedict. 1991. *Imagined Communities: Reflections on the Origin and Spread of Nationalism*. London and New York: Verso.
Atkinson, Paul. 2006. 'Do It Yourself: Democracy and Design'. *Journal of Design History*. 19:10: 1–10.
The Atlantic. 2013. '21 Books Written By and About Women that Men Would Benefit From Reading'. Accessed on 13 May 2013 from www.gq.com/entertainment/books/201304/21-books-for-the-21st-century?currentPage=1.
Australian Bureau of Statistics. 2012. 'Australian National Accounts: National Income, Expenditure and Product, June quarter, 2012'. Report 5206.0.
Australian Communications and Media Authority. 2013. 'Communications Report 2011–12 series: Report 3: Smartphones and Tablets: Take-up and Use in Australia'.
Australian Publishers Association. 2009. 'Australian Book Prices: The Truth'. Accessed on 24 May 2013 from www.ausbooks.com.au/category.php?id=10.
Bailey, John. 2007. 'Magazine City'. *The Age*. 14 October. www.theage.com.au/news/books/magazine-city/2007/10/11/1191696080835.html.
Barthes, Roland. 1973. *Le plaisir du texte*. Paris: Éditions de Seuil.
———.1970. *S/Z*. Paris: Éditions de Seuil.
Batuman, Elif. 2010. 'Get a Real Degree'. *London Review of Books*. 23.
BBC News Europe. 2013. 'Germany Probes Amazon Warehouse Conditions After Film'. February 16. Accessed on 3 May 2013 from www.bbc.co.uk/ news/world-europe-21488816.
Beck, Ulrich. 1994. 'The Reinvention of Politics: Towards a Theory of Reflexive Modernization'. In Ulrich Beck, Anthony Giddens and Scott Lash. *Reflexive Modernization: Politics, Tradition and Aesthetics in the Modern Social Order*. Stanford: Stanford University Press: 1–55.

Beegan, Gerry, and Paul Atkinson. 2008. 'Professionalism, Amateurism and the Boundaries of Design'. *Journal of Design History*. 21:4: 305–313.

Blake, Virgil. 1989. 'The Role of Reviews and Reviewing Media in the Selection Process'. *Collection Management*. 11: 1–40.

Boog Jason. 2011. 'We in the Publishing Business Need to Complain Less.' *GalleyCat*. 28 February. www.mediabistro.com/galleycat/johnny-temple-we-in-the-publishing-business-need-to-complain-less-about-how-no-one-reads_b24282.

Book Industry Strategy Group. 2011. 'Final Report to Government'. September. 17.

Bookseller and Publisher. 2012. 'Nielsen BookScan figures: Overall Sales Down, Top 10 up'. 4 January. www.booksellerandpublisher.com.au.

———. 2012. 'Pre-Christmas Survey 2012: Moderate Expectations.' 19 December. www.booksellerandpublisher.com.au.

Bourdieu, Pierre. 1996. *The Rules of Art*: Genesis and Structure of the Literary Field. Stanford: Stanford University Press.

———. (1986) 2007. 'The Forms of Capital.' In *The Sociology of Education*. Alan Sadovnic, ed. New York: Routledge: 83–96.

———. 2001. *Masculine Domination*. Cambridge: Polity Press.

———. 1993. *The Field of Cultural Production*. Columbia: Columbia University Press.

———. 1990. 'Belief and the Body'. *The Logic of Practice*. Stanford: Stanford University Press: 66–79.

Bradley, Jana et al. 2011. 'Non-Traditional Book Publishing'. First Monday 16:8. 1 August. firstmonday.org/htbin/cgiwrap/bin/ojs/index.php/fm/article/view/3353/3030/.

Braich, Kai. 2012. 'A Look Back at 2012: 10 Things I've Learned From Becoming an Indie Publisher'. *Offscreen*. 29 December. blog.offscreenmag.com/post/39122350182/a-look-back-at-2012-10-things-ive-learned-from.

Brooker, Peter and Andrew Thacker. 2012. *The Oxford Critical and Cultural History of Modernist Magazines*. New York: Oxford University Press.

Brown, Ellen F. 2012. 'Why Book Publishing Can Survive Digital Age'. February 16. Bloomberg Echoes Blog. www.bloomberg.com/news/print/2012-02-16/why-book-publishing-can-survive-digital-age-echoes.html.

Bruder, Jessica. 2011. 'Click, Clack, Ding, Sigh'. *The New York Times*. 30 March. www.nytimes.com/2011/03/31/fashion/31Typewriter.html?_r=0.

Bryant, Nick. 2012. 'The Cultural Creep: Australian Arts on the March'. *Griffith Review*. Winter 36.

Bunting, Catherine et al. 2010. 'Achieving Great Art for Everyone'. United Kingdom: Arts Council.

Cader, Michael. 2013. 'Print Sales Fall Over 9 Percent In US, 3.4 Percent in UK'. January 4. *Publishers Lunch*. lunch.publishersmarketplace.com/2013/01/print-sales-fall-over-9-percent-in-us-3-4-percent-in-uk/.

———. 2012. 'Google And Publishers Settle Long-Running Library Scan Lawsuit'. October 4. *Publishers Lunch*. lunch.publishersmarketplace.com/2012/10/google-and-publishers-settle-long-running-library-scan-lawsuit/.

Carter, David. 2010. 'Transpacific or Transatlantic Traffic? Australian Books and American Publishers'. *Reading Across the Pacific: Australia-United States Intellectual Histories*. Robert Dixon and Nicholas Birns, eds. Sydney University Press.

Carter, David and Galligan, Anne. 2007. 'Introduction'. *Making Books: Contemporary Australian Publishing*. St. Lucia, Queensland: University of Queensland Press.

Case, Jo. 2011. 'Women in Print: an International Women's Day Discussion'. *Kill Your Darlings Blog*. 11 March. www.killyourdarlingsjournal.com/2011/03/women-in-printaninternational-women%E2%80%99s-daydiscussion.

———. 2012. 'Google And Publishers Settle Long-Running Library Scan Lawsuit'. October 'The American Experience'. *The Age*. 17 July. A2: 29.

Catterson, Simon. 2009. 'From Little Ventures Small Wonders Emerge'. *The Age*. January 24. www.theage.com.au/news/entertainment/books/ from-little-ventures-small-wonders-emerge/2009/01/23/1232471568421.html?page=2.

Chell, Elizabeth. 2007. 'Social Enterprise and Entrepreneurship Towards a Convergent Theory of the Entrepreneurial Process'. *International Small Business Journal*. 25:1: 5–26.

Cherland, Meredith. 2008. 'Harry's girls: Harry Potter and the Discourse of Gender'. *Journal of Adolescent & Adult Literacy*. 4:52: 273–282.

Colebrook, Claire. 1997. *New Literary Histories: New Historicism and Contemporary Criticism*. Manchester: Manchester University Press.

Collect. 'About Us'. collectmag.com.au/about/.

Colmer, John. 1971. 'Book Reviewing in Australian Newspapers'. *Meanjin Quarterly*. September. 344–352.

Connor, Michael. 2008. 'How to Rethink Arts Funding'. *Quadrant* 52:10: 5–10.

Cook, Beth et al. 2003. 'Social Entrepreneurship – False Premises and Dangerous Forebodings'. *Australian Journal of Social Issues*. 38:1: 57–72.

Corbett, Steve and Alan Walker. 2012. 'The Big Society: Back to the Future'. *The Political Quarterly*. 83:3: 487–93.

Coronel, Tim. 2012. 'Book Sales Have Fallen Off a Cliff: What Next for the Australian Publishing Industry?' *Island*. 128: 18–26.

Coslovich, Gabriella. 2011. 'Female-Only Literary Prize Puts Gender on the Agenda'. *The Age*. 29 August. www.theage.com.au/entertainment/books/ femaleonly-literary-prize-puts-gender-on-the-agenda-20110828-1jgmy.html.

Couldry, Nick. 2003. 'Media Meta-Capital: Extending the Range of Bourdieu's Field Theory'. *Theory and Society* 32:5/6: 653–677.

Copyright Agency. 2012. 'Copyright Agency reports record numbers copying and sharing Australian content.' December 3. www.copyright.com.au/news/recent-news/ copyright-agency-reports-record-numbers-copying-and-sharing-australian-content.

Crump, S J. 1990. 'Gender and the Curriculum: Power and Being Female'. *British Journal of Sociology and Education*. 11:4:365–385.

Dart, Raymond. 2004. 'The Legitimacy of Social Enterprise'. *Nonprofit management and leadership*. 14:4: 411–24.

Dattner, Zoe. In discussion with Caroline Hamilton.

Davis, Mark. 2010. 'Making Aboriginal History: The Cultural Mission in Australian Book Publishing and the Publication of Henry Reynolds's *The Other Side of the Frontier*'. In *Resourceful Reading: The New Empiricism, eResearch, and Australian Literary Culture*. Katharine Bode and Robert Dixon, eds. Sydney: Sydney University Press: 176–193.

———. 2007. 'The Decline of the Literary Paradigm in Australian Publishing'. In *Making Books: Contemporary Australian Publishing*. David Carter and Anne Galligan, eds. St Lucia: University of Queensland Press: 116–131.

———. 2006. 'The Decline of the Literary Paradigm in Australia.' *Heat* 1:12: 91–108.

Deahl, Rachel. 2010. 'Who's Got Pull in the Publishing Twitterverse'. *Publishers Weekly*. www.publishersweekly.com/pw/by-topic/digital/content-and-e-books/ article/43104-who-s-got-pull-in-the-publishing-twitterverse.html.

Dees, J Gregory. 2007. 'Taking Social Entrepreneurship Seriously'. *Society* 44: 3: 24–31.

Demoor, M et al. 2008. '"And the Winner is?" Researching the Relationship between Gender and Literary awards in Flanders 1981–2001'. *Journal of Gender Studies.* 17:1: 27–39.

Denholm, Michael. 1979. *Small Press Publishing in Australia (The Early 1970s).* North Sydney: Second Back Row Press.

Derricourt, Robin. 2007. 'Book publishing and the university sector in Australia'. *Making Books: Contemporary Australian Publishing.* David Carter and Anne Galligan, eds. St Lucia: University of Queensland Press: 221–230.

Digital Bookworld. 2013. 'Codex Group: Ebooks to Level Off at 30% of Publishing Revenues, With Caveats'. 1 May. Accessed on 23 May 2013 from www. digitalbookworld.com/2013/codex-group-ebooks-to-level-off-at-30-of-publishing-revenues-with-caveats/.

Doctorow, Cory. 2012. 'Doubling Down on DRM'. *Publishers Weekly.* August 13. www.publishersweekly.com/pw/by-topic/columns-and-blogs/cory-doctorow/article/53544-doubling-down-on-drm.html.

Donald, T. 2011. 'How to Turn a Profit from Aussie Film Flops'. *The Punch.* 8 July. Accessed on 11 July 2011 from www.thepunch.com.au/articles/how-to-turn-a-profit-from-aussie-film-flops/.

Donoughue, Peter. 2012. 'Welcome to a World of Pain'. October 31. Pub Date Critical. peterdonoughue.blogspot.com.au/search?updated-max=2012-11-10T10:52:00%2B11:00&max-results=7.

Driscoll, Beth. 2009. 'The Politics of Prizes'. *Meanjin Quarterly.* 68:1: 71–76.

———. 2008. 'How Prizes Work in the Literary Economy'. *HEAT.* 18: 175–194.

———. 2008. 'How Oprah Reinvented the Woman Reader'. *Popular Narrative Media.* 2:2:139–50.

Dunlop, Tim. 2013. *The New Front Page: New Media and the Rise of the Audience.* Melbourne: Scribe.

Duolit. 2012. *Book Marketing Basics: How to Use Facebook, Twitter, Blogging and Email Marketing to Connect With Readers.* Duolit Publishing.

Eagleton, Terry. 1983. *Literary Theory: An Introduction.* Oxford: Blackwell.

Edmonds, Phillip and Dominique Wilson. 2005. Editorial. *Wet Ink* 1:1: 1.

Eisenstein, Elizabeth. 2012. *The Printing Revolution in Early Modern Europe.* Cambridge: Cambridge University Press.

English, J. 2005. *The Economy of Prestige.* London: Harvard University Press.

———. 2002. 'Winning the Culture Game: Prizes, Awards, and the Rule of Art'. *New Literary History.* The John Hopkins University Press. 33:1: 109–135.

Evans, K. 2013. 'Prize Fight has Hidden a Gender'. *The Age.* 13 April. 24.

Falconer, Delia. 2006. 'Risky Proximity'. *Australian Book Review.* August 284: 50.

Fels, Allan. 2009. 'Reading Through the Lines'. *The Age.* 3 July. Accessed on 23 May 2013 from www.theage.com.au/news/opinion/reading-through-the-lines/2009/07/22/1247941959736.html?page=fullpage#contentSwap1.

Fitzpatrick, Nigel. 2012. 'Newspaper Printing or Publishing in Australia'. IBISWorld Industry Report C2421. October.

———. 2012. 'Newspaper and Book Retailing'. IBISWorld Industry Report G4244. November.

Flynn, Chris. In discussion with Caroline Hamilton.

Fowler, Bridget. 2003. 'Reading Pierre Bourdieu's *Masculine Domination*: Notes Towards an Intersectional Analysis of Gender, Culture and Class'. *Cultural Studies* 17:3–4: 468–494.

Fox-Genovese, Elizabeth. 1992. *Feminism without Illusions: A Critique of Individualism*. Chapel Hill: University of North Carolina Press.

Frank, Thomas. 2001. *One Market Under God: Extreme Capitalism, Market Populism, and the End of Economic Democracy*. New York: Anchor.

Freeth, Kate. 2007. 'A Lovely Kind of Madness: Small and Independent Publishing in Australia'. *SPUNC*. November. spunc.com.au/static/files/assets/ae9c26cd/FreethSPUNCReport.pdf.

Frow, John. 1986. 'Class and Culture: Funding the Arts'. *Meanjin* 45:1:118–128.

Gaita, Raimond. 2012. 'To Civilize the City'. *Meanjin* 71:1: 64–82.

Galligan, Anne. 1999. 'Build the Author, Sell the Book: Marketing the Australian Author in the 1990s.' *In Australian Literature & the Public Sphere*, edited by Alison Bartlett, Robert Dixon, and Christopher Lee, 151–158. Toowoomba: ASAL.

———. 2007. 'The Culture of the Publishing House: Structures and Strategies in the Australian Publishing Industry'. *Making Books: Contemporary Australian Publishing*. David Carter and Anne Galligan, eds. St Lucia: University of Queensland Press: 41–43.

Garner, Helen. 2013. 'The Losing Game of Writing to Win'. *The Australian*. 18 May. www.theaustralian.com.au/arts/review/the-losing-gameof-writing-books-to-win/story-fn9n8gph-1226644412788.

Gaughran, David. 2012. 'The Death of Literary Fiction?' *The Huffington Post*, 17 September. Accessed on 23 May 2013 from www.huffingtonpost.com/david-gaughran/the-death-of-literary-fiction_b_1892006.html.

Gay, Roxanne. 2011. 'Too Many of Us, Too Much Noise'. *HTML Giant*. 28 July. htmlgiant.com/random/too-many-of-us-too-much-noise/.

Gelder, Ken and Paul Salzman. 2009. *After the Celebration: Australian Fiction 1989–2007*. University of Melbourne Press.

Gelder, Ken. 2012 'Why Australian Literature Is Alive and Well and Living in Our Universities'. *The Sydney Morning Herald*. 6 May. http://www.smh.com.au/federal-politics/society-and-culture/why-australian-literature-is-alive-and-well-and-living-in-our-universities-20120505-1y5vr.html.

Gilliatt, Tom. (Pan Macmillan). In discussion with Sybil Nolan. October 2012.

Gilmore, Jane. 2012. 'On Paying Writers'. *The King's Tribune*. www.kingstribune.com/index.php/the-shout/item/1599-on-paying-writers.

Giuffre, Giulia. 1987. *To be Australian, a Woman and a Writer*. London: University of London.

Glover, Stuart. 2012. 'Little Magazines, *McSweeney's*, Jordan Bass, and the Future'. 16 October. stuartglover.com.au.

———. 2011. 'No Magazine Is an Island: Government and Little Magazines'. *Island* Summer 127: 21–24.

———. 2007. 'Publishing and the state'. *Making Books: Contemporary Australian Publishing*. David Carter and Anne Galligan, eds. St Lucia: University of Queensland Press: 81–95.

Goldsworthy, Kerryn. 2013. Discussion panel. The Wheeler Centre. 18 April.

Goot, Murray. 1979. 'Newspaper Circulation in Australia 1932–1977'. Media Centre Paper No. 11. Bundoora: Centre for the Study of Educational Communication and Media La Trobe University. 4–9.

GQ. 2013. 'The New Literary Canon: The 21 Books from the 21st Century Every Man Should Read'. Accessed on 12 May 2013 from www.gq.com/entertainment/books/201304/21-books-for-the-21st-century?currentPage=1.

Greco, Albert et al. 2007. *The Culture and Commerce of Publishing in the 21st Century*. California: Stanford University Press.

Grek Martin, Jennifer. 2011. 'Two Roads to Middle-Earth Converge: Observing Text-Based and Film-Based Mental Images'. (Masters), Dalhousie. dalspace. library.dal.ca/handle/10222/14242.

Groden, Michael et al. 2012. *Contemporary Literary and Cultural Theory: The Johns Hopkins Guide*. Baltimore: Johns Hopkins University Press.

Gruzd, Anatoliy and Denel Rehberg Sedo. 2012. 'Investigating Reading Practices at the Turn of the Twenty-First Century'. *Memoires du Livre/Studies in Book Culture* 3:2.

Guthrie, Richard. 2011. *Publishing: Principles and Practice*. London: SAGE Publications.

Habash, Gabe. 2012. 'Twitter and Publishing: How the Industry is Faring in 2012'. *Publishers Weekly*. www.publishersweekly.com/pw/by-topic/industry-news/publisher-news/article/52656-Twitter-and-publishing-how-the-industry-is-faring-in-2012.html

———. 2012. 'How Much Does the Times Book Review Matter?' *Publisher's Weekly*. July 9. 8–9.

Hage, Ghassan. 2000. *White Nation: Fantasies of White Supremacy in a Multicultural Society*. New York: Routledge.

Hall, Donald. 1983. 'Poetry and Ambition'. *The Kenyon Review* 5:4: 90–104.

Hamilton, Caroline. 2011. 'Sympathy for the Devil'. *Overland*. 205: 88–93.

———. 2011. 'On Publishing as a Moral Economy'. *Overland* Summer 205: 88–93.

———. 2011. 'The Exposure Economy'. *Overland* Autumn 202: 88–94.

Hartley, John. 2009. *The Uses of Digital Literacy*. St Lucia: University of Queensland Press.

Harvey, David. 2005. *A Brief History of Neoliberalism*. Oxford, United Kingdom: Oxford University Press.

Hemingway, Christine A. 2005. 'Personal Values as a Catalyst for Corporate Social Entrepreneurship'. *Journal of Business Ethics*. 60:3: 233–49.

Hegarty, Emma. 2006. 'Beyond Bestsellers'. *Paper Empires: History of the Book in Australia, 1946–2005*. Craig Munro and Robyn Sheahan-Bright, eds. St. Lucia, Queensland: University of Queensland Press: 236.

Hegenhan, Laurie. 1986. *The Australian* Short Story: An Anthology from the 1890s to the 1980s. University of Queensland Press.

Henderson, Bill. 1984. 'The Small Book Press: A Cultural Essential'. *The Library Quarterly*. 62.

Hoffert, Barbara. 2010. 'Every Reader a Reviewer'. *Library Journal*. September 1. 22–25.

Holden, Chris et al. 2011. *Social Policy Review 23: Analysis and Debate in Social Policy, 2011*. Policy Press.

Holden, W. Sprague. 1961. *Australia Goes to Press*. Parkville: Melbourne University Press.

Houghton, Greg. *In discussion with Sophie Allan*. Melbourne. 5 June 2013.

Huggan, Graham. 2007. *Australian Literature: Postcolonialism, Racism, Transnationalism*. Oxford University Press.

Humm, Maggie. 1991. *Border traffic*. New York: St Martin's Press.

The Independent. 2012. 'Fifty Shades Of Grey Tops 1m Kindle Sales'. 26 June. Accessed on 23 May 2013 from www.independent.co.uk/arts-entertainment/books/news/fifty-shades-of-grey-tops-1m-kindle-sales-7888760.html.

Indyk, Ivor. 2012. 'Give Baroque Writing a Break'. *The Australian*. 27 October. www.theaustralian.com.au/arts/review/give-baroque-writing-a-break/story-fn9n8gph-1226503179256.

———. 2009. 'Magical Numbers'. *Resourceful Reading: The New Empiricism, eResearch, and Australian Literary Culture*. Katherine Bode and Robert Dixon, eds. Sydney: Sydney University Press: 142–155.

———. 1982. 'Literary Criticism: The Structuralist Controversy'. *Current Affairs Bulletin*. 23–30.

Kakutani, Michiko. 2008. 'A World of Stories from a Son of Vietnam'. *The New York Times*. 18 May. www.nytimes.com/2008/05/13/books/13kaku.html.

Kennedy, Cate. 2012. 'Working with Words'. The Wheeler Centre. 15 November. wheelercentre.com/dailies/post/7a73e588f275/.

Kermode, Frank. 1975. *The Classic*. London: Faber.

Koshland, Ellen. 2013. Discussion panel. The Wheeler Centre. 18 April.

Jacovides, Michael. 2003. 'Love Me, Hate Me … The New World of the Microzine'. *Mag-Culture: New Magazine Design*. Jeremy Leslie, ed. London: Laurence King. 15–17.

Jenkins, Henry. 2006. *Convergence Culture: Where Old and New Media Collide*. New York: New York University Press.

———. 1992. *Textual Poachers*. New York: Routledge.

Johnson, Susan. 2010. 'Measuring the Cultural Cringe'. *The Age*. 22 January. www.smh.com.au/opinion/society-and-culture/measuring-the-cultural-cringe-20100122-mpvs.html.

Lacayo, Richard. 2008. 'Culture Club'. *Time*. January 28.

Laird, Benjamin. 2011. 'Australian Literary Journals: Virtual and Social'. *Cordite Poetry Review*. 1 December. cordite.org.au/features/australian-literary-journals-virtual-and-social/.

Lamond, Julieanne. 2013. 'Stella vs Miles: Women Writers and Literary Value in Australia'. *Meanjin Quarterly*. 71:4: 32.

Lange, Fabian and Robert Topel. 2006. 'The Social Value of Education and Human Capital'. *Handbook of the Economics of Education*. 1: 459–509.

Larsen, Kate. 2013. 'Publishers, You Need to Pay the Writers'. *Overland*.

Lawson, Henry. 1984. *A Camp-Fire Yarn: Complete Works*. Vol 1. Leonard Cronin, ed. Sydney: Lansdowne Publishing.

Lawson, Sylvia. 1983. *The Archibald Paradox: A Strange Case of Authorship*. Allen Lane.

Le, Nam. 2008. *The Boat*. Camberwell: Hamish Hamilton.

Leadbetter, Charles. 2009. *We Think: Mass Innovation, Not Mass Production*. London: Profile.

——— and Paul Miller. 2004. *The Pro-Am Revolution: How Enthusiasts Are Changing Our Economy and Society*. London: Demos.

——— and Kate Oakley. 1999. *The Independents: Britain's New Cultural Entrepreneurs*. London: Demos.

Le Masurier, Megan. 2012. 'Independent Magazines and the Rejuvenation of Print'. *International Journal of Cultural Studies*. 15:4: 383–98.

Lee, Jenny et al. 2009. *The University of Melbourne Book Industry Study 2009*. Melbourne: Thorpe-Bowker: 7.

Lessig, Lawrence. 2004. *Free Culture: How Big Media Uses Technology and the Law to Lock Down Culture and Control Creativity*. New York: Penguin.

———. 2001. *The Future of Ideas: The Fate of the Commons in a Connected World*. New York: Knopf DoubleDay.

Ley, James. 2008. 'No Need for Lesbian Vampires'. *The Age*. 16 June. www.theage.com.au/articles/2008/06/16/1213468314014.html.

Lewis, Wyndham. 1930. *The Apes of God*. The Arthur Press.

Linnell, Garry. In discussion with Matthew Ricketson. November 2012.

Lyons, Martyn. 2001. 'Reading Models and Reading Communities'. *A History of the Book in Australia, 1891 – 1945: A National Culture in a Colonized Market*. St Lucia :University of Queensland Press.

Mair, Johanna and Ignasi Martí. 2006. 'Social Entrepreneurship Research: A Source of Explanation, Prediction, and Delight'. *Journal of World Business*. 41:1: 36–44.

Marchak, M. Patricia. 1991. *The Integrated Circus: The New Right and the Restructuring of Global Markets*. Montreal and Kingston: McGill-Queen's University Press.

Mayr, Suzette and Robyn Read. 2011. 'Collaborations: The Histories and Future of Canadian Creative Writing Programs and Small Press Publishing in Alberta'. *Wascana Review*. 43:1.

MediaFinder. 2013. www.mediafinder.com/.

McEvoy, Mark. 2012. 'Paris Match: Birrell Heads Up Sydney Writers' Festival'. *Sydney Morning Herald*. August. www.smh.com.au/entertainment/books/paris-match-birrell-heads-up-sydney-writers-festival-20120827-24w1l.html.

McGurl, Mark. 2009. *The Program Era: Postwar Fiction and the Rise of Creative Writing*. Cambridge, MA: Harvard University Press.

McLean, Kath and Louise Poland. 2010. *A Case for Literature: The Effectiveness of Subsidies to Australian Publishers 1995–2005*. University of Western Sydney: Writing and Society Research Group (UWS protocol number H7046).

McPhee, Hilary. 2001. *Other People's Words*. Sydney: Picador.

Megalogenis, George. 2012. 'Newman's Axing of Literary Awards Spells Return to Bumpkin State'. *The Australian*. 7 April. www.theaustralian.com.au/national-affairs/newmans-axing-of-literary-award-spells-return-to-bumpkin-state/story-fn59niix-1226320645841.

Menand, Louis. 2009. 'Show or Tell: Should Creative Writing Be Taught?' *The New Yorker*. 8.

Miller, David. 1999. *Principles of Social Justice*. Harvard University Press.

Miller, Laura. 2012. 'In Praise of Nobel Obscurity'. *Salon*. www.salon.com/2012/10/11/in_praise_of_nobel_obscurity/.

Mills, Jennifer and Benjamin Laird. 'Paying the Writers'. *Overland*. 2013.

Mod, Craig. 2010. 'Books in *The Age* of the iPad'. @craigmod. March. craigmod. com/journal/ipad_and_books/.

Moi, Toril. 1991. 'Appropriating Bourdieu: Feminist theory and Pierre Bourdieu's sociology of culture'. *New Literary History* 22:1019–49.

Morrison, Elizabeth. 1998. 'A Fourth Estate Down Under: How Newspapers in the British Mould Dominated Colonial Australian Print Culture'. *Epilogue*. 13: 29–40.

———. 1988. 'Press Power and Popular Appeal: Serial Fiction and *The Age*, 1872–1899'. Media Information Australia. August: 49–52.

Morrison, Ewan. 2011. 'Are Books Dead, and Can Authors Survive?' 22 August. Accessed on 23 August 2011 from www.guardian.co.uk/books/2011/aug/ 22/are-books-dead-ewan-morrison?intcmp=239.

Mort, G.S. et al. 2003. 'Social Entrepreneurship: Towards Conceptualisation'. *International Journal of Nonprofit and Voluntary Sector Marketing*. 8:1: 76–88.

Moylan, Michelle and Lane Stiles. 1996. *Reading Books: Essays on the Material Text and Literature in America*. Amherst: University of Massachusetts Press.

Mumbrella. 2012. 'Nicole Sheffield CEO of Expanded NewsLifeMedia …' 2 March.

Naas, Michael. 2008. *Derrida from Now On*. New York: Fordham University Press.

Nielsen BookScan Australia. 29 May 2013. In discussion with Mark Davis.

Nile, Richard and David Walker. 2001. 'The "Paternoster Row Machine" and the Australian Book Trade, 1890–1945'. *A History of the Book in Australia 1891–1945: A National Culture in a Colonised Market*. Martyn Lyons and John Arnold, eds. St Lucia: University of Queensland Press.

Nobel Prize for Literature. 2013. Accessed on 7 August 2013 from www.nobelprize. org/alfred_nobel/biographical/articles/erlandsson/.

O'Brien, Connor Tomas. 2013. "Likes' Don't Pay the Rent'. *Kill Your Darlings*. www. killyourdarlingsjournal.com/2013/07/likes-dont-pay-the-rent/.

O'Connor, Sarah. 2013. 'Amazon Unpacked'. *Financial Times Magazine*. 8 February. Accessed on 24 May 2013 from www.ft.com/cms/s/2/ed6a985c-70bd-11e2-85d0-00144feab49a.html#slide0.

Omundsen, Wenche and Michael Jacklin. 2008. *Mapping Literature Infrastructure in Australia: A Report to the Australia Council for the Arts' Literature Board*. 4–5. University of Wollongong/Australia Council.

O'Reilly, Nathanael. 2009. 'A Stunning Debut from a Remarkable New Talent'. *Antipodes*. June. 93–94.

O'Reilly, Tim. 2005. 'What is Web 2.0? Design Patterns and Business Models for the Next Generation of Software'. O'Reilly Media. www.oreilly.com/pub/a/oreilly/ tim/news/2005/09/30/what-is-web-20.html.

Osborne, David. 1993. 'Reinventing Government'. *Public Productivity & Management Review*. 349–56.

Overland. 2013. 'About Us'. overland.org.au/about/.

Page, Jon. 2012. 'A New Form of Price Gouging?' November 13. *Bite the Book: Book Reviews and Industry Views*. bitethebook.com/2012/11/13/a-new-form-of-price-gouging/.

———. 2011. 'Book Pricing – Repeating the Same Mistakes Only On a Bigger Scale'. *Bite the Book: Book Reviews and Industry Views*. 8 September. Accessed on 23 May 2013 from bitethebook.com/2011/09/08/book-pricing-2/.

Pearson, Jacqueline. 1999. *Women's Reading in Britain 1750–1835: A Dangerous Recreation*. Cambridge: Cambridge University Press.

Peredo, Ana Maria and Murdith McLean. 2006. 'Social Entrepreneurship: A Critical Review of the Concept'. *Journal of World Business*. 41:1: 56–65.

Pilkington, E. 2012. 'Amanda Hocking, the Writer Who Made Millions by Self-Publishing Online'. 12 January. Accessed on 11 November 2012 from www. guardian.co.uk/books/2012/jan/12/amanda-hocking-self-publishing.

Phillips, A.A. 2012. 'The Cultural Cringe'. *The Words that Made Australia*. Robert Manne and Chris Feik, eds. Collingwood: Black Inc. Agenda.

PricewaterhouseCoopers Australia. 2011. *Cover to Cover: A Market Analysis of the Australian Book Industry*. Canberra: Department of Innovation, Industry, Science and Research. Accessed on 9 May 2013 from www.innovation.gov.au. /Industry/ BooksandPrinting/BookIndustryStrategyGroup/Documents/PwCCovertoCover. pdf.

Puplick, Chris. 2008. *Getting Heard: Achieving an Effective Arts Advocacy*. Strawberry Hills: Currency House (Platform Papers No. 18).

Pykett, Lyn. 1992. *The 'Improper' Feminine: The Women's Sensation Novel and the New Woman Writing*. London; New York: Routledge.

Randall, D'Arcy. 2012. 'Seven writers and Australia's literary capital'. *Republics of Letters: Literary Communities in Australia*. Peter Kilpatrick and Robert Dixon, eds. 204–216.

Reed, Jon. 2011. *The Publishing Talk Guide to Twitter*. Reed Media.

Reich, Robert. 2008. *Supercapitalism: The Transformation of Business, Democracy and Everyday Life*. Melbourne: Scribe.

Reimer, Andrew. 2008. 'The Boat'. *Sydney Morning Herald*. 20 June. www.smh.com. au/news/book-reviews/the-boat/2008/06/20/1213770909981.html.

Riddell, Sheila. 1992. *Gender and the Politics of the Curriculum*. London: Routledge.

Robinson, Colin. 2012. 'Ten Ways to Save the Publishing Industry'. *The Guardian*. www.guardian.co.uk/books/2012/oct/12/ten-ways-to-save-publishing-industry.

Rosenbloom, Henry. 2012. 'Deconstructing Penguin House'. October 31. Scribe Publications News and Events. scribepublications.com.au/news-and-events/ post/deconstructing-penguin-house/.

Rowling, J.K. 2013. Accessed on 9 July 2013 from www.jkrowling.com.en_ US/#timeline/pen-name/.

Rowse, Tim. 1985. *Arguing the Arts: The Funding of the Arts in Australia*. Ringwood: Penguin.

Rubbo, Mark. 2012. 'Future for Writers and Publishers Linked to Bookselling'. *The Age*. 16 July. Accessed 17 July 2012 from www.theage.com.au/opinion/ society-and-culture/future-for-writers-and-publishers-linked-to-bookselling-20120715-2242y.html.

Ryan, Colleen. 2013. *Fairfax: The Rise and Fall*. Carlton, Victoria: Miegunyah Press.

Ryan, Roxy. (Hardie Grant Books). In discussion with Sybil Nolan. October 2012.

Schumpeter, Joseph. 1975. *Capitalism, Socialism and Democracy*. New York: Harper.

Scott, Ronnie. In discussion with Caroline Hamilton.

Sedgmann, Jayne-Maree. 2004. 'Miles Franklin Judges Resign After Spat With Trust'. Accessed on 10 February 2013 from www.abc.net.au/am/content/2004/ s1270275.htm.

Seymour, Liz. In discussion with Caroline Hamilton.

Shatzkin, Mike. 2012. Trying to Explain Publishing, or www.Understand It, Often Remains a Great Challenge'. October 31. *The Shatzkin Files*. idealog.com/ blog/2012/10/.

Shergold, Peter. 2011. 'Seen But Not Heard'. *The Australian*. 4 May.

Sheridan, Susan. 2012. '"Opposing All the Things They Stand For": Women Writers and the Women's Magazines'. *Republics of Letters: Literary Communities in Australia*. Peter Kilpatrick and Robert Dixon, eds. 195–204.

Sherk, Adam. 2010. '10 Practical Twitter Tips for Publishers'. Adam Sherk. www. adamsherk.com/social-media/Twitter-tips-for-publishers/.

Shirky, Clay. 2008. *Here Comes Everybody: The Power of Organizing Without Organizations*. London and New York: Penguin Books.

Shivani, Anis. 2010. 'Creative Writing Programs: Is the Mfa System Corrupt and Undemocratic?' *The Huffington Post*. www.huffingtonpost.com/anis-shivani/ creative-writing-programs-corrupt_b_757653.html.

Silverman, Jacob. 2012. 'Against Enthusiasm: The Epidemic of Niceness in Online Book Culture'. *Slate*. 4 August. www.slate.com/articles/arts/books/2012/08/ writers_and_readers_on_twitter_and_tumblr_we_need_more_criticism_less_ liking_.html.

Singer, Peter. 2010. *The Life You Can Save: Acting Now to End World Poverty*. Melbourne: Text Publishing Company.

Skidelsky, William. 2008. 'Critical Condition'. *Prospect*. February. 32–36.

Sparrow, Jeff. 2013. 'Editorial'. *Overland*. Winter 2013.

Steger, Jason. In discussion with Matthew Ricketson. November 2012.

Stephens, Mitchell. 1997. *A History of News*. Fort Worth: Harcourt Brace.

WORKS CITED

Stinson, Emmett. 2012. 'Critical Danger: Book Reviewing, Prizes and Australia's Literary Consensus-Culture'. *The Wheeler Centre Dailies*. 28 August. wheeler centre.com/dailies/post/b6d4b3141c8f/.

———. 2011. 'Vanity Fair: Why Traditional Publishers Need to Take Self-Publishing Seriously'. *Overland* 204 (Spring): 63–70.

Street, John. 2005. '"Showbusiness of a Serious Kind": a Cultural Politics of the Art Prize'. *Media, Culture and Society*. 27:6: 819–840.

Sullivan, Jane. 2009. 'Damn the Doom…' *The Age*. 11 July.

———. 2006. 'Back to Her Roots'. *The Age*. 16 September. www.theage.com.au/news/books/back-to-her-roots/2006/09/14/1157827093579.html.

Sumara, D. 1998. 'Fictionalising Acts: Reading and the Making of Identity'. *Theory into Practice*. 37:3: 203 –210.

Swinn, Louise. 2013. Lecture. The University of Melbourne. 8 April 2013.

———. (Sleepers Publishing). In discussion with Sybil Nolan. November 2012.

Tacon, Dave. 2009. 'Finding a Home in Fiction'. *The Age*. 31 October. www.theage.com.au/articles/2009/10/30/1256835150139.html.

Tan, W.L. et al. 2003. 'What Is the Social in Social Entrepreneurship?' Singapore Managament University.

Taste.com.au. 2010. 'Taste Newspaper Liftout now Weekly'. February. www.taste.com.au

Thompson, John B. 2012. *Merchants of Culture: The Publishing Business in the Twenty-First Century* (2nd Edition). New York and London: Plume.

———. 2010. *Merchants of Culture* (1st Edition). Cambridge: Polity Press. 187–222.

Thorburn, David and Henry Jenkins. 2003. 'Introduction: Toward an Aesthetics of Transition'. *Rethinking Media Change: The Aesthetics of Tradition*. Cambridge: MIT Press: 1–17.

Trachtenberg, Jeffrey A. 2013. 'Publisher Makes TV Play'. *The Wall Street Journal*. 18 August. online.wsj.com/article/SB10001424127887323455104579017242094248698.html.

Tuchman, Gaye. 1989. *Edging Women Out: Victorian Novelists, Publishers, and Social Change*. New Haven: Yale University Press.

Twyford-Moore, Sam. 2012. 'Letter from Australia'. *The Los Angeles Review of Books*. 25 June. lareviewofbooks.org/article.php?id=717&fulltext=1.

VCAL. 2013. Accessed on 2 May 2013 from www.vcaa.vic.edu.au/Pages/vcal/index.aspx.

VIDA. 2013. Women in Literary Arts. Accessed on 29 April 2013 from www.vidaweb.org/.

Wallace, Diana. 1998. '"Writing as Re-vision": Women's Writing in Britain, 1945 to the Present Day'. *An Introduction to Women's Writing: from the Middle Ages to the Present Day*. M Shaw, ed. Hertfordshire, Great Britain: Prentice Hall. 235–263.

Westbury, Marcus. 2009. 'Evolution and Creation: Australia's Funding Bodies'. *Meanjin* blog. July. Accessed on 29 October 2012 from meanjin.com.au/blog/post/evolution-and-creation-australia-s-funding-bodies/.

Wilding, Michael. 1978. 'The Tabloid Story Story'. *The Tabloid Story Pocket Book*. Sydney: Wild & Woolley.

Williamson, Geordie. 2012. *The Burning Library: Our Great Novelists Lost and Found*. Melbourne: Text Publishing.

———. 2010. 'Writing to Win'. *The Australian*. 3 February. www.theaustralian.com.au/arts/books/writing-to-win/story-e6frg8nf-1225825444846.

Wilson, Sean. In discussion with Caroline Hamilton.

Wyndham, Susan. 2012. In discussion with Matthew Ricketson.

Zangen, Britta. 2003. 'Women as Readers, Writers, and Judges: The Controversy about the Orange Prize for Fiction'. *Women's Studies*. 32: 281–299.

Zizek, Slavoj. 2010. *Living in the End Times*. London and New York: Verso.

———. 2009. *First as Tragedy, Then as Farce*. London: Verso.

Zwar, Jan. 2012. 'What Were We Buying? Examining Non-fiction and Narrative Non-fiction Reading Patterns in the 2000s'. *Journal of the Association for the Study of Australian Literature*. 12:3. Accessed on 12 August 2013 from: www.nla.gov. au/openpublish/index.php/jasal/article/view/2446/334.

CONTRIBUTORS

Sophie Allan is completing a Master of Publishing and Communications at the University of Melbourne. She is the editor of *Plane Tree*, the University of Melbourne Graduate Student Association's biannual magazine, and works as a freelance writer and copyeditor.

Professor Kevin Brophy teaches Creative Writing in the School of Culture and Communication at the University of Melbourne. He has been part of Five Islands since 2007. He is author of twelve books of poetry, fiction and critical essays. In late 2013 John Leonard Press will publish a 'New and Selected' edition of his poetry.

Tim Coronel is an editor, writer and publishing consultant. He was editor and publisher of Thorpe-Bowker's *Books+Publishing* from 2002–2011 and editor of and contributor to the *University of Melbourne Book Industry Study 2009*. He is currently co-ordinating the 2013 Independent Publishers Conference for the Small Press Network.

Mark Davis is the author of *The Land of Plenty: Australia in the 2000s* (MUP 2008) and *Gangland: Cultural Elites and the New Generationalism* (Allen & Unwin 1997, 1999). He teaches in the School of Culture and Communication at the University of Melbourne.

Peter Donoughue retired from the publishing industry in March 2009, after a 35-year career in the Australian book trade. His last position was Managing Director of John Wiley and Sons Australia Ltd, a role he held for sixteen years. He held numerous industry positions during his career, including President of the Australian Publishers Association (1996/1997) and a Director of CAL (1993–2003). In recent years Peter has made a particular study of digital publishing, including ebooks, and has written extensively on these and related issues.

Beth Driscoll is a Lecturer in Publishing and Communications at the University of Melbourne. She researches contemporary literary culture, and has published articles on Oprah's Book Club, the Man Booker Prize and the uses of Harry Potter in literacy education. She is preparing a monograph on the new literary middlebrow.

Phillip Edmonds lectures in Australian Literature and Creative Writing at Adelaide University. For seven years he was the co-managing editor of *Wet Ink: The Magazine of New Writing*, which published a host of up-and-coming authors and attempted to set up a new, independent model for literary magazines in Australia. Phillip is also the author of eight books, including the novella, *Leaving Home with Henry* (2010). He is currently concluding work on a history of Australian literary magazines between 1969 and 2012.

Amy Espeseth is a writer, publisher and academic, who has published widely and is the recipient of many prizes and awards. Her first novel, *Sufficient Grace*, received critical and popular acclaim in 2012; her second novel, *Trouble Telling the Weather*, will be published in 2014. She lectures in both writing and publishing at NMIT.

Caroline Hamilton is a McKenzie Research Fellow in Publishing and Communications at the University of Melbourne. During 2013 she is visiting fellow with the Institute for Advanced Studies in publishing at the University of London. She is the author of *One Man Zeitgeist: Dave Eggers, Publishing and Publicity* (Continuum, 2010).

Ivor Indyk is founding editor and publisher of *HEAT* magazine and the award-winning Giramondo book imprint, and Whitlam Professor in the Writing and Society Research Group at the University of Western Sydney. A critic, essayist and reviewer, he has written a monograph on David Malouf for Oxford University Press, and essays on many aspects of Australian literature, art, architecture and literary publishing. He is one of the founders of the *Sydney Review of Books*.

Aaron Mannion is Associate Publisher at Vignette Press. He has edited and co-edited a range of publications including the creative writing anthology *Muse*; the Australasian Association of Writing Program's anthology, *Nth Degree*; the reviews section of *Traffic*, and, most recently, Vignette Press's *Geek Mook*. He teaches creative writing and editing.

Dr Sybil Nolan is a lecturer in publishing and communications at the University of Melbourne, with a background in both daily journalism and publishing. She has worked for *The Australian* and *The Age*, and was a commissioning editor at Melbourne University Publishing from 2003 to 2007.

Dr Matthew Ricketson is an academic and journalist. In 2009 he was appointed the inaugural professor of journalism at the University of Canberra. Before that he was Media and Communications editor for *The Age*. He is the author of a biography of Australian author, Paul Jennings, and a textbook about journalism. He has edited an anthology of profiles and most recently *Australian Journalism Today*.

Emmett Stinson is a Lecturer in Publishing and Communications at the University of Melbourne. He was a co-founder and former President of the Small Press Network. He was also a co-founder and Fiction Editor of *Wet Ink: The Magazine of New Writing* (2005–2012). His collection of short fiction, *Known Unknowns* (Affirm Press, 2010), was shortlisted for the Steele Rudd Award as part of the Queensland Literary Awards. With Richard Pennell and Pam Pryde, he co-authored *Banning Islamic Books in Australia* (Melbourne University Publishing, 2011).

EDITOR'S ACKNOWLEDGMENTS

I would like to express my utmost gratitude to Sophie Allan, Duncan Campbell-Avenell and Sarah Couper – three students in the Masters of Publishing at the University of Melbourne, who copyedited and formatted this manuscript. Without their efforts, putting this book together would not have been possible.

I would also like to thank Nathan Hollier, both for helping me to convene the inaugural Academic Day of the Independent Publishing Conference in 2012 and for his support in publishing this collection. I would also like to thank everyone else at Monash University Publishing for their assistance in putting this book together.

Finally, I would like to thank Zoe Dattner and the Board of the Small Press Network for their help in organising the Independent Publishing Conference, without which this publication would not have existed.

PUBLISHING ACKNOWLEDGMENTS

An earlier version of Tim Coronel's 'What Next for the Australian Book Trade?' was published in the Autumn 2012 issue of *Island Magazine* as 'Book Sales Have Fallen Off a Cliff'. An earlier version of Sybil Nolan and Matthew Ricketson's 'Unintended Consequences' appeared on February 22, 2013 in *The Sydney Review of Books* as 'Parallel Fates'. An earlier version of Emmett Stinson's 'In the Same Boat' was published on March 26, 2013 in *The Sydney Review of Books*.